DICTIONARY OF
HAMMOND-ORGAN STOPS

An Introduction to Playing the Hammond Electric Organ

and a Translation of Pipe-Organ Stops into

Hammond-Organ Number-Arrangements

By

STEVENS IRWIN

Completely Revised Edition, containing New Sections

on the Pedal Solo Unit and the Hammond Spinet

G. SCHIRMER, INC., NEW YORK

The need of a "Dictionary" for the Hammond Organ tone qualities has become increasingly apparent as the use of the instrument has spread into homes, churches, schools, theaters, and public auditoriums. The musical amateur as well as the experienced organist, in exploring and employing the vast gamut of tone colors of which the instrument is capable, is confronted with a great volume of published organ literature in which the indications for the conventional organ registrations must be translated into the new symbols adopted for the Hammond Organ. The "Dictionary" will serve as a quick and easy reference book for this purpose, furnishing equivalents for organ stops in terms of the new instrument.

The compiler of this book is an experienced player and exponent of the Hammond Organ. In the course of his compilation he has submitted his manuscript for our examination and we have tested many of the tonal combinations listed therein for their fidelity. We commend this book to the use of anyone interested in cultivating a comprehensive knowledge of the tonal resources of the Hammond Organ.

HAMMOND INSTRUMENT COMPANY
Chicago

INTRODUCTION

This Dictionary of Hammond-Organ Stops has been compiled to form a "bridge" between the conventional pipe-organ stops and the Hammond Organ. The Harmonic Controllers of the Hammond Organ create tonal possibilities of which the organ-builder of the past would not have dared to dream.

As the artist has the three fundamental colors—blue, yellow, and red—at his command, the organist now has nine fundamental colors of the sound "spectrum". These he can mix in millions of different proportions, and thus obtain any shade or hue in a whole immense range of sound. Trumpet tone and Violin tone are merely different colors in the sound world. They may be obtained by mixing their component parts in certain proportions. These proportions are the subject of this Dictionary.

Just as the color orange is a mixture of red and yellow, Clarinet tone is a mixture of its components. However, there are many shadings of Clarinet tone, just as there are many shadings of orange. But the ear in determining the difference between these different shadings of sound is perhaps more precise than the eye in determining the difference between shadings of color.

When a pipe-organ builder builds a Clarinet stop into a pipe-organ, he gives the organist a choice as to whether the Clarinet is to be bright or dull in tone. When the organ is erected, the Clarinet is finished; it cannot be changed. It can be turned on or off: that is the limit of its versatility. On the Hammond Organ, on the other hand, the organist can voice his stops at the console. He voices them at the same time as he draws them. He can make his Clarinet either bright or dull at the time he draws the Clarinet stop. And the same applies to all of the stops of the organ.

Great dynamic range is possible on the Hammond Organ. When the Expression Pedal is depressed, the volume of the Clarinet, for example, can be made to equal a ten-rank Clarinet. Instant changes are also possible in the volume of the Electric Organ. A Full Organ can be reduced to a whisper as fast as the foot can be moved. There is no waiting for a Swell Box to close.

Instant response is obtained from the keys of the Electric Organ. The fraction of a second needed to cause a pipe to speak, on the pipe-organ, is for practical purposes eliminated. Pipes thirty-two feet in length require a second or more to speak; the corresponding tones of the Electric Organ speak instantly. This is a decided advantage in rapid pedal passages.

On the Electric Organ, a small cube less than a yard in dimension can produce more variety in stops than a large pipe-organ which would take up twenty very large rooms around the sides and top of a stage. The power of such an organ could also be simulated by adding several of these cubes to the console.

With all these features to its advantage the Electric Organ takes its place in usefulness in all kinds of organ work beside the most carefully-voiced pipe-organ.

This Dictionary should prove useful to the experienced organist as well as to the beginner. It is as devoid as possible of technical terms. But it would be impossible to depart from organ language without taking away from the value of the Dictionary. If the beginner who is unacquainted with stop-names will draw the stops and listen to them for the purpose of associating them with their names, he will soon find that the few difficulties of language which are a beginner's in any technical subject will disappear. The experienced organist will find here a basis upon which to begin his association with the Electric Organ. He will see familiar names all through the book and will marvel that so many different varieties of a single stop are possible, and that he has his choice among them.

The compiler of this Dictionary has been guided by:

1. Dictionaries of organ stops, especially that of George Ashdown Audsley, which is very precise in its descriptions;

2. Standard works on the construction of the pipe-organ;

3. Books, pamphlets, and stop-lists of many organ companies from both this country and abroad;

4. Special attention to the timbres of stops heard in organs both in this country and abroad, especially in cathedrals.

Various organ-builders have their own ideals of the tonal requisites of each stop. Standards in Europe differ from those in this country. The writer, too, has his ideals, and he has tried to keep them conservative and according to good organ tradition. If the reader has a different ideal for the timbre of a certain stop-name, he can realize his ideal merely by manipulating the Harmonic Controllers. In this way a tone altogether suited to his tastes can be produced.

A few of the stops in this Dictionary were taken from the literature of the Hammond Organ. Credit is due to the manufacturers for these number-arrangements. The illustrations of this book are also reproduced with the kind consent of the makers of the Electric Organ.

It has been thought necessary to cover in this Introduction *some* of the same ground that is covered by the Elementary Instruction Book published by the manufacturers, entitled "Playing the Hammond Organ". But it is assumed that the user of this Dictionary has already read that book.

CONTENTS

Page

INTRODUCTION.. v
THE USE OF THIS DICTIONARY.. 3
THE HARMONIC CONTROLLERS... 4
NUMBER-ARRANGEMENTS AS ORGAN STOPS............................... 6
BASIC NUMBER-ARRANGEMENTS.. 8
NUMBER-ARRANGEMENT ENDINGS....................................... 12
COMBINING STOPS.. 13
THE PRE-SET KEYS... 14
THE TREMULANT.. 18
THE CHORUS CONTROL... 18
THE EXPRESSION PEDAL... 21
THE PEDAL HARMONIC-CONTROLLERS................................... 22
THE PEDAL SOLO UNIT.. 23
PLAYING THE PEDAL KEYBOARD....................................... 25
THE ACCOMPANIMENT OF VOICES...................................... 26
THE ORGAN WITH ORCHESTRA OR BAND................................. 28
ACOUSTICS AND THE ORGAN.. 29
MAIN TONE GENERATOR.. 31
THE HAMMOND SPINET... 33

THE DICTIONARY:

THE FOUNDATION STOPS... 36
THE REED STOPS... 48
THE FLUTE STOPS.. 73
THE STRING STOPS... 78
THE FULL ORGANS.. 90
THE PERCUSSIONS.. 91
SUGGESTED SELECTIONS FOR THE AVERAGE ORGANIST.................... 92

ILLUSTRATIONS

FIGURE 1. DIAGRAM OF THE PARTS OF THE HAMMOND-ORGAN CONSOLE...... 2
FIGURE 2. THE HARMONIC CONTROLLERS.............................. 5
FIGURE 3. TYPICAL HAMMOND-ORGAN MANUALS......................... 5
FIGURE 4. VOLUME AND VIBRATO CONTROLS ON MODELS B-2, C-2, RT-2;
            PEDAL SOLO UNIT ON MODELS RT, RT-2.................. 19
FIGURE 5. THE PEDAL KEYBOARD.................................... 24
FIGURE 6. TONE GENERATOR.. 32
FIGURE 7. THE HAMMOND SPINET.................................... 34

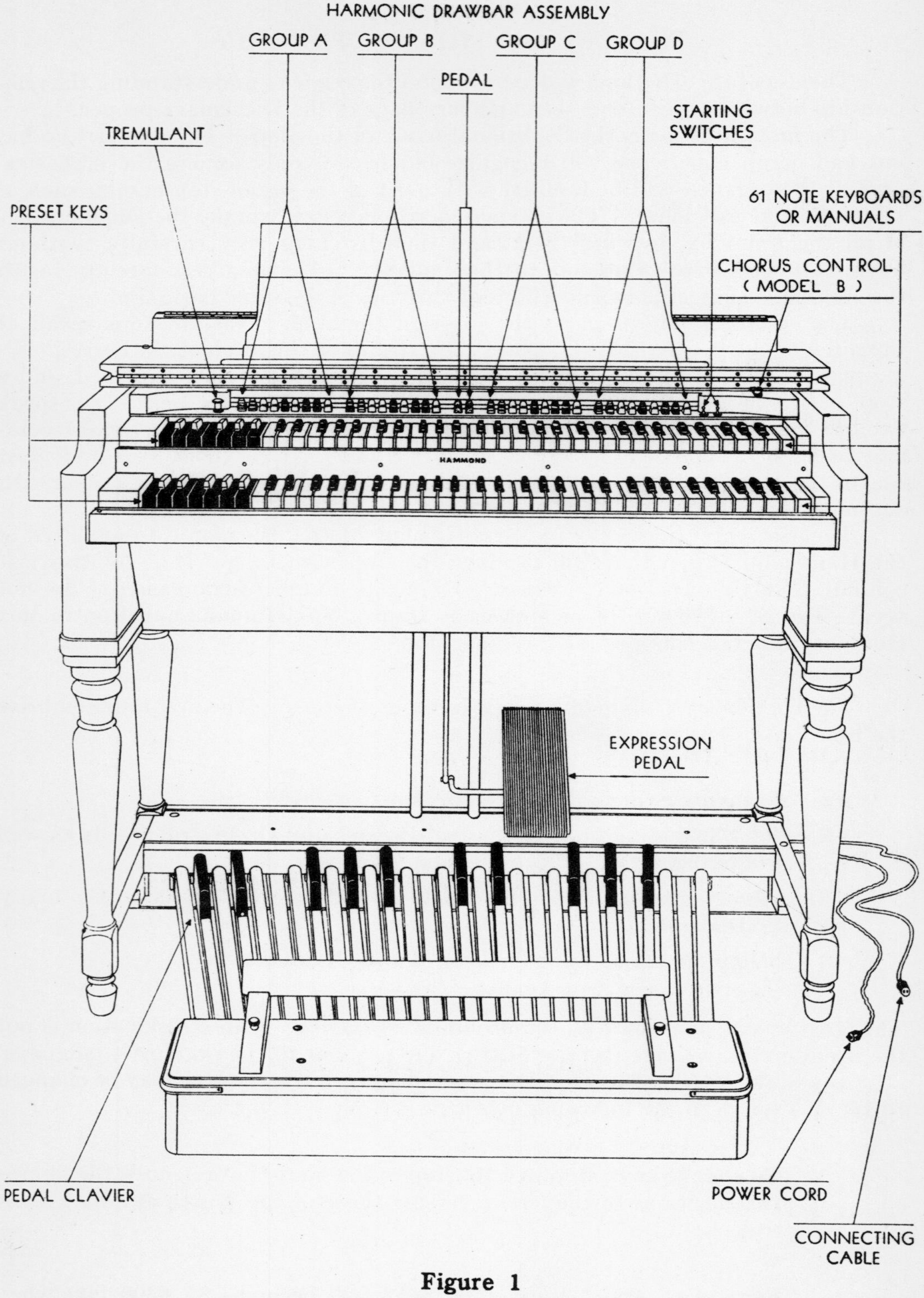

HARMONIC DRAWBAR ASSEMBLY

GROUP A   GROUP B   GROUP C   GROUP D

PEDAL

STARTING
SWITCHES

TREMULANT

61 NOTE KEYBOARDS
OR MANUALS

PRESET KEYS

CHORUS CONTROL
(MODEL B)

HAMMOND

EXPRESSION
PEDAL

PEDAL CLAVIER

POWER CORD

CONNECTING
CABLE

Figure 1

Diagram of the Parts of the Hammond-Organ Console

2

THE USE OF THIS DICTIONARY

The use of this Dictionary depends upon the reader's understanding the relationship between three items seen on every page of the Dictionary proper.

The first entry gives the traditional name of the stop. The reader who has not had organ experience will recognize old friends only among the orchestral names; the organist will be familiar with most of the organ stop-names, such as Diapason and Salicional. The inexperienced player may make the acquaintance of all the tones by drawing them, and then listening very carefully (without Tremulant or Chorus Control) to their quality. The numbers directly below the stop-names merely identify different varieties of the same basic timbre.

The second entry indicates the pitch of the stop. Not all stops speak at the pitch of the key depressed. An 8' stop speaks at the pitch of the corresponding piano key. A stop marked 16' speaks one octave lower than expected, and a stop marked 4' speaks one octave higher than expected. Other stops speak two or even three octaves above, or at the other pitches given in the table accompanying the chapter on the Harmonic Controllers. Everybody will find most use for the 8' stops. The professional organist will want to supplement them with considerable use of the stops of higher and lower pitch.

The last entry indicates the arrangement of the Harmonic Controllers of the Hammond Organ that will produce the indicated tone. It is for this last column that this Dictionary exists. Duplicate number-arrangements do not occur—except, of course, in such cases as Double Vox Humana and Contra Vox Humana, which are names for the same stop.

The Dictionary is divided into six divisions of stops. The first four comprise the four families of organ tone. They are:

1. *Foundation*, including all Diapasons;

2. *Reed*, including both Orchestral Brasses and Orchestral Reeds as well as the regular organ-type Reeds;

3. *Flute*, including the Orchestral Flute and Piccolo, as well as the many Flutes peculiar to the organ world;

4. *String*, including both Orchestral and Organ Strings.

The last two divisions are *Full Organs* and *Percussions*. This classification is not the usual orchestral classification, but is one peculiar to the organist's language.

Any of the stops in this Dictionary which are given at 8' pitch may be changed to 16' or 4' pitch in the following manner:

1. To change an 8' stop to a 16' stop of the same timbre, move the figures two positions to the left, reversing those of the fourth and fifth Controllers;

   Example: An 8' stop of 00 8653 000 becomes 85 6300 000 when changed to a 16' stop.

2.   To change an 8' stop to a 4' stop of the same timbre, move:

    a.   the third Controller figure one position to the right,
    b.   the fourth Controller figure two positions to the right,
    c.   the fifth Controller figure three positions to the right,
    d.   the sixth Controller figure three positions to the right;

Example: An 8' stop of 00 8653 000 becomes 00 0806 053 when changed to a 4' stop.

Thus any one of the 8' stops of the Dictionary may become a stop of another pitch (one octave lower or one octave higher), but does not lose its timbre in the change.   However, the ear is most sensitive to timbre around the center of the keyboard, and the very low and very high stops seem to lose their qualities when played at the extreme ends of the keyboard.

THE HARMONIC CONTROLLERS

The Harmonic Controllers are located in four identical groups above the keys. The groups from left to right are lettered A, B, C, and D.   The first two are for the operation of the upper manual, and the third and fourth for the operation of the lower manual.   The two Pre-Set keys (B♭ and B) operate, in the manner of a switch, the respective groups belonging to their manuals.   Only one Pre-Set group can be played at a time because only one Pre-Set key can be depressed at a time.   Either a Pre-Set combination or a Harmonic-Controller combination must be used.   The Pre-Set combinations are set up in the back of the console, and are semi-permanent; the Harmonic-Controller combinations are set up by the organist at the time of playing, and are temporary.

Each of the Harmonic Controllers governs a pure, colorless tone.   It is only when the Controllers are drawn in combination with each other that a tone similar to that of a Trumpet or Violin is made.   Nine different positions are available for each Harmonic Controller.   There are eight speaking positions and the "off" position.   The "off" position is very important in some stops, such as a Clarinet arranged in this fashion: 00 5160 310.   The zero (denoting the "off" position) is very seldom used in the midst of larger figures; it usually appears at the left or right ends of the number-arrangements.

Proportion plays an important part in using the numbers stamped on the Controllers.   The arrangement 00 2400 000 is identical in timbre to 00 1200 000, but there is a difference in volume.   The former is the louder because of the larger figures.   But 00 1200 000 could be made as loud as 00 2400 000 by depressing the Expression Pedal.

It is by combining *pitch* and *volume* in various ratios that different tone-colors are obtained.   This whole Dictionary is merely a balanced collection of these tone-colors, governed by the Harmonic Controllers.

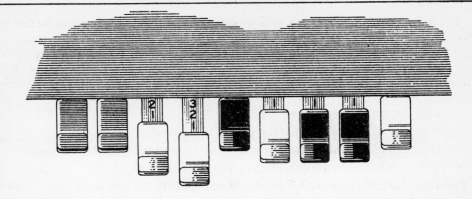

I II III IV V VI VII VIII IX

The Harmonic Controllers

Figure 2

The Harmonic Controllers of the Electric Organ are
illustrated drawn to the number-arrangement
00 2301 110

The Harmonic Controllers from left to right are as follows:

	Color	Name	Speaking Pitch	Note which sounds when middle C is played
I	Brown	Sub-octave	16'	octave below
II	Brown	Fifth	5⅓'	fifth above
III	White	Unison	8'	middle C
IV	White	Octave	4'	octave above
V	Black	Twelfth	2⅔'	octave and fifth above
VI	White	Super-octave	2'	two octaves above
VII	Black	Seventeenth	1⅗'	two octaves and third above
VIII	Black	Nineteenth	1⅓'	two octaves and fifth above
IX	White	Super-Super-octave	1'	three octaves above

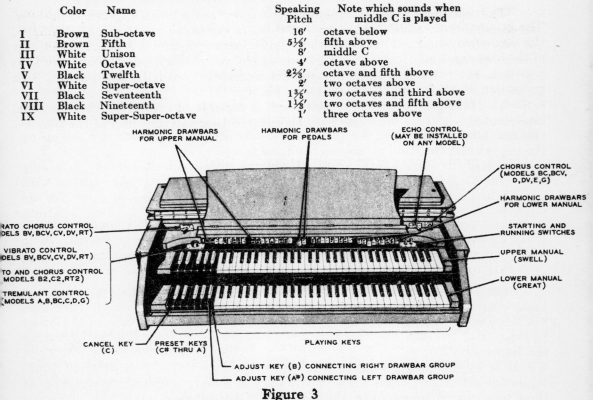

Figure 3
Typical Hammond-Organ Manuals
(See also Fig. 4, p. 19)

Each of the nine Harmonic Controllers may be said to have a distinct influence on the tone to which it is added. The descriptive statements which follow are to be interpreted only generally, because of the many exceptions to them. However, they will interest the organist who likes to make his own Controller arrangements. The Harmonic Controllers are named from left to right:

I   —adds depth to any stop;

II   —adds a dull, metallic quality useful in powerful stops;

III   —adds fundamental power to any stop (the most useful Controller);

IV   —adds brightness and carrying power to any stop;

V   —adds the String and Orchestral Reed quality to any stop;

VI   —adds brilliance to any stop;

VII —adds a "Brass" quality when drawn in large proportion to the other Controllers, and a "String" quality when in small proportion;

VIII—adds the octave of V (Useful to supplement VII, but usually in smaller proportion than VII);

IX   —adds great brilliance (to be used only in Full Organ combinations, or as the ending of String "curves"; exceptions to this rule are rare).

NUMBER-ARRANGEMENTS AS ORGAN STOPS

The newcomer to the Hammond Organ is confronted with a system of number-arrangements by which all the known stops of the organ world can be simulated on any Hammond. This system of number-arrangements is a graphic and easy means of manipulating the four groups of Harmonic Controllers above the keys of the organ. Each of these number-arrangements is usually accompanied by a traditional name, such as Diapason or Violin.

The four groups are alike, and each is capable of producing the full tonal range of the organ. Any one may be selected to create the stop of the player's choice.

A typical number-arrangement looks like this:

00 6644 310

All number-arrangements are divided, for the sake of ease of vision and analysis, into groups of two, four, and three figures. The first group consists of the Controllers producing 16' and 5⅓' tone; the second group contains the Controllers referred to in this book as "basic"; the third group constitutes the "ending".

In obtaining the tone of one of these number-arrangements, it is necessary to do the following:

1.   Draw out the Controllers of any one of the four groups, in the order indicated in the number-arrangement, to the point where the desired figures are just visible in front of the frame above the Controllers. The Controllers which are represented by a "zero" should be left "in" completely so that the first number, which is "1", is not visible;

2. Depress the Pre-Set key corresponding to the Harmonic-Controller group of the manual which is being used to create the stop selected (see Fig. 3). The Controllers are lettered from left to right A, B, C, and D. Groups A and B are for the upper manual and are obtained respectively by Pre-Set keys A♯ and B. Groups C and D are for the lower manual and are obtained respectively by Pre-Set keys A♯ and B (see Fig. 1).

It is necessary to have nine different Controllers for each stop because each tone of the musical world consists not of a single sound but of a complicated group of sounds. If Violin tone is desired, a correctly-proportioned group of Controllers must be drawn. This proportion is indicated by the number-arrangement. Trumpet tone has a different number-arrangement. The same applies to all other timbres. Some tones have all the Controllers in use, and some only a few.

With the Harmonic Controllers the beginner can make simple experiments, and the more advanced student of registration can experiment almost endlessly. The beginner should learn first how to draw the most important stops—those of which many varieties are given in this Dictionary. The advanced student should branch out boldly, using his own judgment and imagination in making number-arrangements. This, however, should not be done until he has mastered the fundamentals of drawing all the most important stops. The number-arrangements in the Dictionary may be amplified and changed by the advanced student; very few players will want to be completely guided by these number-arrangements.

Some general rules are here set down for those whose interest carries them beyond this Dictionary:

1. Don't waste time making number-arrangements which have no musical value. Of the more than 387,000,000 possibilities, many have no interest to either the player or the listener. Such an arrangement as 18 4368 285 is distorted in timbre to the point where it is unnatural and uninteresting. You would not mix blue, yellow, and red in a paint-box carelessly; you would try to obtain from them a definite hue, value, and saturation. Do the same with the fundamental colors of the sound "spectrum".

2. Determine the pitch of the stop you are making. If it is an 8' stop (as beginners' stops should always be), make the third Controller of any one of the four groups the basis of your number-arrangement.

3. In general, make the Controller figures recede to the right. It is one of nature's laws that overtones (harmonics) recede in this fashion.

4. Study the chapter entitled "Basic Number-Arrangements".

5. Learn to listen carefully; the ear is more reliable as a guide to timbre than is generally realized. Visit other organs than your own (those in churches, theaters, and radio studios), listening to the timbres of the stops you hear; try to simulate them on your own organ.

6. At the ends of the four tonal divisions of the Dictionary, a few unassigned number-arrangements are given. Apply the names which you believe fit most precisely those tones in which you are interested.

It is probable that if every possible variety of every basic pattern in this Dictionary were worked out, the number of stops resulting would be in the neighborhood of 74,000,000, each one being a variety of some traditional stop. But to the master patterns upon which the more than 3,500 stops listed in this Dictionary are founded, only a few could be added which would not duplicate one given here. (The String division is the greatest field for the student searching for new stops, and the Reed division the second greatest). After each of the more important stop-names in this Dictionary, space has been left in which the student may record number-arrangements that he has discovered for himself.

The traditional resources of the Hammond Organ may be summarized in the following list, which represents a conservative choice of the stops built upon the main fundamental designs of basic number-arrangement.

Open, Harmonic, and Horn Diapasons	8, 421 stops
Gemshorns	212,521 stops
Tubas and Trumpets	107,004 stops
Clarinets	478,979 stops
French Horns	211 stops
Saxophones	8,100 stops
Flutes	2,455 stops
Strings (including Orchestral Wood-winds)	265,997 stops
Full Organs and Reed Choruses	22,986,392 stops
Vox Humanas	74,088 stops
String Organs	23,407,399 stops
16'	12,380,060 stops
8'	12,380,060 stops

(The Clarinets are not included in the Orchestral Wood-winds because their fundamental design is different from that of other Wood-winds, which is the same as that of the Strings.)

BASIC NUMBER-ARRANGEMENTS

This short description of the basic or master number-arrangements is the key to this Dictionary. All the facts of this chapter should be retained in the memory.

There are four major families of organ tone. Each has a typical number-arrangement. There are also other less important basic number-arrangements, which have been included for the sake of completeness.

The four families of organ tone are as follows:

I	Foundation	00 8855 000	(Open Diapason)
II	Reed	00 8888 000	(Tuba)
III	Flute	00 8400 000	(Flute)
IV	String	00 1374 000	(Orchestral String)

There are many amplifications and variations of these four general patterns, but the majority of the stops in this Dictionary are based on these four configurations.

The Foundation stops of the organ are usually Diapasons. The tone of the Diapason is the most suitable organ tone for the accompaniment of the human voice. Organ solos are usually played on the Diapasons. All of the poets' praise of the "pealing" organ belongs to the Diapasons. The Diapasons have a distinctly organ tone, and do not imitate any orchestral instrument. It is heavy and sometimes dull in quality, which fits it well for works whose texture is mostly in chords.

The typical Foundation arrangement is:

00 8855 000

The word Open in the name Open Diapason refers to the open metal pipe which is required in the pipe-organ to give Diapason tone. It need not confuse the reader. The first two Controllers are in the zero position. The next four Controllers appear in pairs of receding strength towards the right. Any number-arrangement in which these four Controllers are paired thus, with the second pair weaker than the first, produces some sort of Diapason tone. All of the following are for this reason Diapasons:

00 8877 000
00 8811 000
00 7744 000
00 6633 000
00 2211 000

Added brightness can be given to any Diapason by adding the seventh and eighth Controllers in receding strength. Thus our typical Diapason may become:

00 8855 310

The Reed tones are more brilliant and more numerous than any other family of stops. They are the solo stops of the organ. Very seldom is a Reed used for purposes of accompaniment.

A Reed tone as somber as a Diapason or one as piercing as an Orchestral Trumpet can be produced on the Controllers. It is possible to make a Trumpet even more piercingly brilliant than any naturally blown Trumpet. This is possible by the building-up of the tone on the Harmonic Controllers.

The typical Reed may be produced by the number-arrangement:

00 8888 000

The first two Controllers are at zero, as they usually are. The next four are equal in strength. Brightness could be added to the Reed by adding the seventh and eighth Controllers in receding strength, as in the Diapason just considered:

00 8888 310

This would, however, not be as bright in tone as a Tuba generally is.   A better arrangement would be:

00 8888 750

A typical Trumpet is based on the typical Tuba Reed above, but has less of the fundamental (third Controller), thus:

00 7888 750

An even more piercing Trumpet could be made in this fashion:

02 5788 850

The second Controller has been added, to give "clang" to the tone.   The third and fourth Controllers have been weakened, to make the tone less heavy.   Heaviness makes the stop seem like a Tuba, which is the organ world's name for a powerful organ Reed tone.

Other important Orchestral Reeds are the English Horn, Oboe, and Clarinet. They are remarkably like the Orchestral Violin in harmonic structure.   Definite distinctions should be made:

Oboe	00 1271 210
English Horn	00 3471 210
Clarinet	00 6170 310
Orchestral Violin	00 1374 321

The fundamental (third Controller) of the English Horn is always stronger than that of the Oboe.   The fundamental of the Clarinet is always as strong, or almost as strong, as its fifth Controller.   The sixth Controller of the Clarinet is absent in the foregoing arrangement.   It should be absent or very weak in all Clarinets. It is even possible to suggest a Clarinet tone in the following combination:

00 6060 000

The essence of the Clarinet tone will be seen to consist of just the fundamental and the fifth Controller tone.

The Orchestral Violin has its sixth Controller in great prominence.   This adds the quality known as brightness to all Strings.

The accompaniment stops of the organ are the Flutes.   Being of a more or less colorless quality, they lend themselves to chorded backgrounds.

A typical Flute tone is:

00 8400 000

This example is of an open, unstopped pipe. A more powerfully-blown Open Flute would become:

00 8532 000

In this number-arrangement two additional harmonics appear. The figures recede to the right rather sharply.

A Stopped Flute pipe has as its lowest harmonic the fifth Controller tone (the twelfth):

00 6020 000

The fifth Controller is always much weaker than the third Controller in such a stop.

The String stops are the most versatile of all the four major divisions of organ tone. They can be used as both solo and accompanimental stops. String tone is nearly always formed on a number-arrangement which appears as a "curve":

00 1374 321

The apex of the curve is reached at the twelfth, or fifth Controller. There are many hundreds of basic number-arrangements of String curves, and the entire range of them could be made to be either dull or bright-toned Strings by varying the sharpness of the curve.

A Gemshorn tone, although not a String, is closely related to a String. A typical Gemshorn appears:

00 4531 000

The foregoing rules are indispensable in understanding the Harmonic Controllers of the Electric Organ. They have been reduced to the minimum. An entire volume might be devoted to the amplifications of these rules and the exceptions to them.

It is necessary to realize that proportion is the essential thing in all these number-arrangements. The arrangements:

00 8400 000
00 4200 000
00 2100 000
00 6300 000

all have the same timbre, because the fundamental in all cases is twice the strength of the Controller following it. It is not possible to take such a combination as:

00 5300 000

and diminish each Controller one point and have the same timbre. If we did so, the above combination would become:

00 4200 000

The reader can easily see that these two combinations are of a different proportion, and will therefore produce a different timbre. Don't make the common error of diminishing all the Controllers of an arrangement one point, expecting to keep the same timbre.

NUMBER-ARRANGEMENT ENDINGS

The following number-arrangement endings are given in the order of their increasing brilliance. They may be added to any of the unassigned number-arrangements found at the end of the divisions of Foundation, Reed, and String tone in the Dictionary. They could also be added to the other stops in these three divisions of the Dictionary in preference to those given by the writer, if they are more in keeping with the player's musical taste.

The figures, of course, represent the positions of the last three Controllers in each number-arrangement (given in the unassigned lists as 000). Care should be taken to use an ending which is not too brilliant for the stop in question. In general, the first figure of the ending should not be greater than the last figure of the basic arrangement.

The Flute division does not require additional endings to its timbre, as Flute tone is comparatively free of the higher harmonics.

The endings are as follows:

000	440	770	333	543	653	751	811	864
100	510	810	411	544	654	752	821	865
200	520	820	421	551	655	753	822	866
300	530	830	422	552	661	754	831	871
400	540	840	431	553	662	755	832	872
500	550	850	432	554	663	761	933	873
600	610	860	433	555	664	762	841	874
700	620	870	441	611	665	763	842	875
800	630	880	442	621	666	764	843	876
110	640	111	443	622	711	765	844	877
210	650	211	444	631	721	766	851	881
220	660	221	511	632	722	771	852	882
310	710	222	521	633	731	772	853	883
320	720	311	522	641	732	773	854	884
330	730	321	531	642	733	774	855	885
410	740	322	532	643	741	775	861	886
420	750	331	533	644	742	776	862	887
430	760	332	541	651	743	777	863	888
			542	652	744			

The most important endings, as the reader has probably observed, are in the first half of the list. The endings in the second half of the list should be used with caution, and added to a basic number-arrangement only when it will not make the listener more conscious of the ending than of the original timbre of the stop.

The most useful ending is 210. It will become the favorite ending of most players in Foundation, Reed, and String tones.

After a short experience with the Hammond Organ, the player will select his own endings. They should be suited to the acoustic conditions of the room in which the speaker is placed. In general, the larger the room, the more brilliant all stops will have to be. Great auditoriums with ceilings over one hundred feet in height will require endings producing the greatest brilliance; churches of moderate size will require endings in keeping with their size; small living rooms and funeral parlors will require the least brilliance. Experience with full and empty halls is the best teacher in selecting the appropriate ending for all stops.

COMBINING STOPS

When registration instructions call for a single stop to be drawn on a particular manual, it is a simple matter to create that stop with the Harmonic Controllers. When the registration instructions call for two, three, or four stops, the combining of these stops so that they are all produced by one number-arrangement is less simple. There is, however, a method of doing this that will achieve good results for the organist.

Let us combine:

00 5543 210

00 8020 000

The resultant number-arrangement is made up of the higher figure for each Controller in either arrangement. The greater figure for each of the first two will be 0. For the third Controller, 8, of course, is greater than 5. The remaining figures of the upper arrangement are all greater than their counterparts in the lower, and therefore they make up the rest of the arrangement:

00 8543 210

Here is an example of this method applied to the combining of three stops into a single arrangement which will sound like all of them being played together. Let us combine these three:

01 6788 540

00 8210 000

00 1354 321

Each of these will contribute some figures to the resultant:

01 8788 541

To combine a great many stops according to this same method requires quite an increase in volume, as several stops, even though of the quiet type, augment the volume when added together. Therefore it is necessary to depress the Expression Pedal as nearly as possible in proportion to the increase in volume that the addition of several stops would naturally produce.

Let us combine six stops representing all four main families of organ tone:

00 2100 000
00 1444 310
01 7651 310
00 3564 321
02 8888 886
00 7744 100

The resultant arrangement is:

02 8888 886

This arrangement is, of course, identical with the powerful Reed tone which is next to the last in the group. It can be said that Reed tone contains within its harmonic structure Diapason, Flute, and String tones as component parts of its make-up. Likewise, Diapason tone contains Flute tone (and sometimes String tone) as a component part of its make-up.

All Full-Organ tones are similar to the most powerful Diapasons or Reeds, as the most powerful stop of an organ dominates the Full-Organ tone almost completely. The mind of the listener is unaware of the sounding of the many softer stops, because it is centered in the dominating tone. Nevertheless the softer stops add to the general volume of the Full Organ.

In making arrangements of the Controllers to create Full-Organ tone, it is only necessary to choose a powerful Reed or Diapason arrangement and add to it an appropriate amount of 16' tone. Sometimes the addition of a little 1' tone will give the impression of an unusually large Full Organ. Care should be taken to avoid too much 1' tone even in Full Organs.

The Mixtures of a pipe-organ are identical with the upper harmonics of the Reeds, and should not stand out unduly in the attention of the listener. A typical Full-Organ arrangement which has been created from all four classifications of organ tone is:

63 8888 856

Any number of stops in this Dictionary can be combined in a single number-arrangement. The Expression Pedal must always be taken into consideration in creating the effect of a very great Full Organ. Perhaps the addition of more power cabinets will be necessary to satisfy the player's ideal of a Full Organ. The registration-instructions of any piece of music can be followed, regardless of how many stops the author desires combined. Two stops or a dozen or more can be combined by the same method.

THE PRE-SET KEYS

The Pre-Set keys furnish a means of drawing certain fixed number-arrangements without having to set each Harmonic Controller individually. Thus they correspond to the stops on a pipe-organ, and also, as we have just seen, to the Combination Pistons on such an organ.

The Pre-Set keys are located at the left-hand ends of the two manuals. There are two groups, one governing each manual.

A large part of the stop-drawing will be done by these Pre-Set keys. The use of the Pre-Set keys Bb and B has been explained (p. 4). Those from C#

to A, inclusive, are set up in semi-permanent fashion from the back of the console, but may be changed at the will of the organist. However, it is necessary to have a service man make such changes. It would not seem undesirable in some cases for a careful, mechanically-minded person to learn how to make them. But they are somewhat complicated, and call for careful, patient work. In case the organist desires a new set-up on his Pre-Set controls, he should make a list showing Harmonic Controllers in the strengths wanted and names of Pre-Set keys in their alphabetical order, and either give it to a service man or make the necessary adjustment himself.

Any stop given in this Dictionary could easily be set up on any Pre-Set key. An organist could also go through the Dictionary selecting his whole group of Pre-Set keys in any possible order he might desire.

The use of the Pre-Set keys is very simple. When the organist is about to become acquainted with the organ for the first time, he should obtain a chart showing which stops are set on the various Pre-Set keys. The memorization of this chart is very easy, probably not more than one hour's actual playing of the organist's most familiar pieces would be required to achieve complete familiarity with it. If the organist desires to learn the chart quickly, five minutes of con- centrated effort will probably teach it to him.

After acquaintance with the Pre-Set system is established, the player should turn his attention to the Harmonic Controllers. When sitting down to play the organ, most organists adjust the Harmonic Controllers as well as the Pre-Sets. There being only nine Pre-Sets on each manual, a favorite Tuba or Orchestral Wood-wind is frequently not provided. These favorite stops, as well as some needed accompanimental Flutes, must be set before playing, as fifteen seconds are usually required in making one adjustment of the Harmonic Controllers. Quick changes of stops must be effected by the Pre-Sets. Therefore it is necessary to set the desired combination on the Harmonic Controllers (if it is not on one of the Pre-Sets) before the selection is begun. A quick change is always to be antici- pated and provided for before the first note of the selection is struck.

The "C" Pre-Set keys on both manuals are cancels for any other Pre-Set on the same manual. If two Pre-Sets are depressed by mistake, the cancel should be used to release them. In changing from one Pre-Set to another, it is not necessary to use the cancel; one Pre-Set releases another.

The motion required to actuate a Pre-Set key is directly downward, and never to either side. A firm, carefully-directed stroke is sure to cause the key to remain depressed. This is important; for it is most embarrassing to make a thrust at a key in the pause between phrases of a selection, only to find that the manual keys are being depressed without causing the organ to play, since the Pre-Set key has not been firmly depressed. Firmness and care in manipulating the Pre-Set keys are necessary to a smooth performance. A very quick motion may be developed by practice. In some players the motion in depressing a Pre- Set key is so well anticipated that it seems subconscious.

Never depress more than one Pre-Set key at a time.

After the organist has become familiar with the organ, he may desire a differ- ent Pre-Set arrangement. Several such arrangements are here presented, with a few notes in regard to their particular type of usefulness. All of the following stops were taken from the Dictionary.

Players of classical organ works will find the following set-up to their tastes. Diapason tone is in large proportion to the other tones.

Upper Manual

C♯	Open Flute	00 7510 000
D	Dulciana	00 3330 000
D♯	French Horn	00 7642 000
E	Salicional	00 2453 210
F	Stopped Flute	00 5020 000
F♯	Oboe (organ type)	00 3561 210
G	Swell Diapason	00 7765 410
G♯	Trumpet (organ type)	00 7677 540
A	Full Swell Organ	73 8888 542

Lower Manual

C♯	'Cello	00 1444 321
D	Major Flute	00 6430 000
D♯	Bell Clarinet	00 6173 310
E	Tuba	00 6888 760
F	Open Diapason No. 1	00 8855 100
F♯	Open Diapason No. 2	00 5522 100
G	Diapason Chorus No. 1	82 8855 325
G♯	Diapason Chorus No. 2	61 8855 541
A	Full Great Organ	84 8888 854

The following arrangement of the Pre-Set keys is intended for the organist who likes to play famous symphony themes, arias, and other parts from favorite operas. The Dulciana has been repeated in the Lower Manual because of its excellent accompanimental tone:

Upper Manual

C♯	Stopped Flute	00 5020 000
D	Dulciana	00 2220 000
D♯	English Horn	00 2481 310
E	French Horn	00 7642 000
F	Saxophone	01 8761 310
F♯	French Trumpet	00 7888 750
G	Keraulophone	00 6432 000
G♯	Keen Strings	00 1475 331
A	Full Orchestral Organ	87 8888 677

Lower Manual

C♯	Stopped Flute	00 5010 000
D	Dulciana	00 2220 000
D♯	'Cello	00 1444 321
E	Orchestral Flute	00 3821 000
F	Clarinet	00 4160 321
F♯	Tibia Dura	00 8410 000
G	Tuba Mirabilis	00 8888 850
G♯	Full Accompanimental	31 6666 432
A	Diapason Chorus	82 8855 324

The person who enjoys playing hymns and familiar songs will enjoy having the following Pre-Set stops on his organ:

Upper Manual

C#	Stopped Flute	00 5020 000
D	Dulciana	00 2220 000
D#	String Organ No. 1	22 5787 321
E	String Organ No. 2	23 4767 100
F	French Horn	00 7642 000
F#	English Horn	00 2481 310
G	Clarinet	00 4160 321
G#	Cathedral Diapason	00 7755 100
A	Full Swell Organ	86 8888 453

Lower Manual

C#	'Cello	00 1444 321
D	Tibia Clausa	00 8020 000
D#	Unda Maris	00 2430 000
E	Echo Diapason	00 3322 000
F	Open Diapason	00 8855 100
F#	Fanfare	01 4888 850
G	Stentorphone	00 8640 000
G#	Ethereal Violin	00 1242 100
A	Full Great Organ	74 8888 431

The reader whose particular interest is in registration could make up additional tonal schemes for his Pre-Set keys.

A larger model of the Hammond Organ (known as Model E) has round, numbered pistons in place of the standard Pre-Set keys herein described. They serve the same purposes and are adjustable in the same manner as the Pre-Set keys, to which they correspond as follows:

Models A and B Pre-Set Keys	Model E Pre-Set Pistons
C	0
C#	2
D	1
D#	4
E	3
F	5
F#	6
G	7
G#	8
A	9
Bb	10
B	11

THE TREMULANT

The Tremulant is controlled from the left side of the console by a small, round knob. It is completely in the "off" position when turned far to the counter-clockwise. By moving it in the clockwise direction by very small degrees, an almost imperceptible tremolo is obtained at first. As the knob is turned farther, the tremolo gradually increases. The organist can stop the knob at any point he desires, and thus have a constant tremolo.

In general, it is better not to use the Tremulant with Diapasons. Its use should be restricted to the more delicately-voiced stops. However, the Open Diapason, being a very useful solo voice, might be employed with the Tremulant to advantage.

Any Diapason Chorus should be played without the Tremulant. The sound of a tone without the Tremulant will seem to be louder than the same tone with the Tremulant. All Full Organs should be played without the Tremulant.

The emotional character of the music being played is the best guide for the player's use of the Tremulant. The individual player will have to form a set of standards of his own in regard to the Tremulant. The style of playing and the type of music played will both have much to do with these standards.

The Tremulant is a special device for special purposes. It should be a matter of musical "morals" not to use this device without reason.

The Tremulant can be used in some cases to compensate for lack of reverberation time in a small room. The effect is, however, purely psychological: it draws the listener's attention to the effect of the Tremulant and away from the lack of reverberation.

The degree of tremolo to be used should be as carefully chosen as the times for the use of the Tremulant. A large room can absorb more tremolo than a small room. Certain selections can carry more tremolo than others. And there is a definite correlation between harmony, timbre, and melody, and the use of the Tremulant. Some selections just naturally need the Tremulant.

Hymns, unless of a pensive, quiet nature, should be played without the Tremulant. Staccato passages and strident melodies with powerful accompaniments should also be played without the Tremulant.

Authorities on organ playing differ in their attitude towards the use of the Tremulant. Some advocate its use frequently; others condemn it. The contemporary standard for its use seems to be to tolerate it except in the most classical or most strictly liturgical types of music.

THE CHORUS CONTROL

At the right side of the console is a single controller that looks like the other Harmonic Controllers. It is marked "Chorus". When drawn, it changes all the stops of the organ into *célestes*.

Organists know a *céleste* tone as one which undulates pleasantly, and so rapidly that the ear cannot hear the individual beats. This type of tone is for certain purposes more pleasant to both trained and untrained ears than the normal, single-pitched tone more frequently heard.

A *céleste* is obtained by sounding two, three, or more pitches for the same note at the same time, all of which, when sounding simultaneously, give the listener the impression that he is hearing only one note, which wavers almost imperceptibly in a way that is pleasant to the ear. The listener with a sense of absolute pitch is not offended by the *céleste* type of tone.

The counterpart of the *céleste* tone is found in the string section of the symphony orchestra. The violins, although carefully tuned, have separate pitches. For all of the violins to be in perfect, absolutely-true pitch with each other is impossible. Slipping pegs and stretching strings, not to mention human imperfections, prevent this.

When the sound waves from the violins mingle, a wavering is set up, which, because of the closeness of the pitches, is very rapid; so rapid that the listener is not specifically aware of it.

The magical strains of the "Grail Theme" in Wagner's opera "Lohengrin" bear the charm they do partly because of this phenomenon of undulation. In fact, all of the instruments of the orchestra, all of the ranks of pipes in an organ, and all of the voices of a choir or chorus undulate. Constantly perfect pitch for all of the sounding bodies of any ensemble is impossible.

If the organ player will hold down middle C and the C♯ beside it, he will hear three things: the vibrations of the two notes and a beating besides, which is a resultant effect. This is discord to the senses. If the pitch of the C♯ were so close to that of the C that the listener could not tell the difference in the pitches, there could be a difference, nevertheless, which would cause an indefinite, wavering effect. The *céleste* principle takes advantage of this fact.

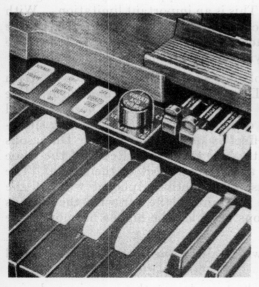

Figure 4-A
Models B-2, C-2, and RT-2 have Volume and Vibrato Controls illustrated.

Figure 4-B
Models RT and RT-2 have Pedal Solo Control Unit illustrated above.

Public musical standards have forced the organ industry to manufacture instruments purposely which undulate as *célestes*. One violin does not have the same quality as ten violins because the undulating factor is missing. Absolutely true, unwavering pitch is unsatisfactory to most people.

A pipe-organ *céleste* is formed by causing two or more pipes to speak simultaneously when a single stop is drawn and a single key is depressed.

If the *céleste* is added to a tone already sounding, the listener has the impression merely that the tone has been made to undulate—not that a new tone has been added, as he would if (let us say) an Oboe were added to a Diapason.

The *céleste* principle of the Electric Organ is that of the three-rank *céleste* of the pipe-organ. Flat, sharp, and normal pitches are heard when the Chorus Control is drawn. When it is not drawn, each note speaks at only one pitch.

Older models are provided with a Chorus Generator, an electrical unit built into the console of the organ. A knob turns it off and on when the *céleste* effect is desired. Continuously with the true pitch, the Chorus Generator both flats and sharps the pitch at the same time. As low pitches do not need any undulation, the middles and right-hand ends of the two keyboards are affected only. At the center of the keyboards the variation from true pitch is only eight-tenths of one percent; at the right-hand ends of the keyboards the variation from true pitch is much less, only four-tenths of one percent. It is musically desirable that less rapid undulation be present near the top of the scale.

On the Electric Organ the Chorus Control permits Diapason, Reed, Flute, and String tone each to be instantly modified on the *céleste* principle. On the conventional pipe-organ, the *céleste* principle can be applied only to String and Flute tone, and then only to a few stops. This is an important limitation. With the Trumpet, for example, there is a decided advantage in having the *céleste* attachment; it imparts a "silvery" character to the tone, and also makes the impression that several Trumpets are playing instead of one.

The Chorus Control should invariably be used with String stops. With Flute stops it may or may not be used. Diapason tones sound more nearly like their pipe-organ counterparts without it. However, adding the Chorus Control gives the illusion that at least three ranks of Diapason pipes are speaking simultaneously. The most "cathedral-like" effect is obtained from the Diapasons without the Chorus Control or Tremulant. The Orchestral Reeds of the Oboe type need the Chorus Control to impart a wavering effect to their tone. The heavy Chorus Reeds, such as the Tubas, are effectively played without the Chorus Control, although they are more pleasant to the ear with the Chorus Control, which seems to make all loud stops in which the higher harmonics are strong more natural in tone.

The stops in the Dictionary proper which always need the Chorus Control are marked with an asterisk.

When both Chorus Control and Tremulant are drawn, the organ is producing two wavering effects in the tone at the same time. The Tremulant produces actual waves in the pitch of each tone produced. The Chorus Control creates the impression of such waves as the result of a slight mis-tuning of tones which are individually perfectly steady.

It is not right or wrong to turn the Chorus Control "on" or "off". All of the above rules may be disregarded without seeming to play incorrectly, but when followed they will ordinarily make the playing of the organ more effective from a standpoint of timbre.

On the newer models of the Hammond Organ there is a Selective Vibrato system which permits the organist to achieve independently a vibrato effect on either or both of the manuals and pedals. For example, a Violin solo may be played with a vibrato on the upper manual with a contrasting non-vibrato Wood-wind accompaniment on the lower manual. Both the Great and Swell manuals are provided with separate "On-Off" vibrato controls in the form of tilting stop tablets. Next to these tablets is a rotating "Vibrato and Chorus" control with six positions corresponding to the three degrees of Vibrato and three degrees of Vibrato Chorus (the latter a mixture of vibrato and non-vibrato tones). This control pre-selects the extent of vibrato or vibrato chorus obtained when the vibrato "On-Off" stop for either or both manuals is used. The vibrato effect for the pedal is controlled by the same stop as the Great.

THE EXPRESSION PEDAL

The Expression Pedal is one of the greatest friends of the organist. It enables him to make a general accompanimental tone, such as 00 8742 000, soft enough to accompany a child's voice, or loud enough to accompany a whole congregation.

The Expression Pedal makes the volume of any stop on the organ louder or softer. Actual "steps" of volume could be heard if the ear were sensitive enough. But the differences in volume between the many "steps" are so numerous and minute that increase or decrease of volume is accomplished without noticeable jumps.

In the pipe-organ it is possible to obtain from one stop-rank only the amount of volume that one rank of pipes can give. By means of the electric Expression Pedal, which operates in a manner similar to a rheostat, it is possible to draw a String tone such as 00 1444 210 with the Expression Pedal in the soft position and obtain volume equal to a fraction of that one rank of pipes. When the Expression Pedal is depressed, this fraction grows slowly to a volume equal, sometimes, to that of ten ranks of pipes. In the case of a loud Tuba it would grow to only two or three ranks of pipes.

Any powerful agent of expression is likely to be absurd at times, and the Expression Pedal is no exception. One way of abusing it is to "pump" it. An "expression pumper" is an organist who makes the organ become louder and softer frequently and without any reason for doing so implied in the music itself.

The Expression Pedal is the easiest device on the organ console with which to become acquainted. The novice obtains satisfaction from its use immediately.

The dynamic markings of the music to be played can be followed minutely with the Expression Pedal. *Sforzando* effects on any stop can be obtained instantly with it. Its action is instantaneous.

It is a mistake to startle the senses of the listeners by striking a chord suddenly on a powerful stop with the Expression Pedal open. If the first chord of a selection must be of highest intensity, it is best to have the Expression Pedal in a fairly soft position when the chord is struck, and then it can be depressed so quickly that the listener hears a powerful organ almost at once but has not been startled.

THE PEDAL HARMONIC-CONTROLLERS

The two Harmonic Controllers for the Pedal-board are located between the groups of manual Controllers B and C. The Controller at the left is the more frequently used. When drawn by itself it produces a tone on the Pedal-board similar to the Bourdon stop of a conventional pipe-organ. This Controller is sufficient, when drawn by itself, for ordinary quiet, unpretentious playing. When Diapasons, Reeds, or Full Organs are used, the right Controller should be drawn with the left. The degree to which it should be drawn will depend upon the proportions of the tone used on the manuals. If the manual-stop used is very brilliant, the proportion of the right Controller to the left should be as three to four. If the tone on the manuals is milder, the proportion of one to four would be sufficient.

The Controller at the left produces a tone made up mostly of the fundamental. There is a small amount of octave and twelfth in it as well. The Controller at the right contains no less than four additional overtones. These overtones are graduated in strength in such a manner that they cannot be individually heard.

Below are given several examples of Pedal combinations which balance (under ordinary acoustical conditions) the manual combinations beside them.

Manual		Pedal
Echoflöte	00 2100 000	10
Dulciana	00 2220 000	20
Echo Violin	00 1243 210	30
Horn Diapason	00 4443 210	40
Gamba	00 3484 431	31
Open Diapason	00 6644 310	41
Open Diapason	00 8844 200	42
Tuba Sonora	02 7788 650	73
Diapason Chorus	82 8855 323	85
Reed Chorus	83 8888 872	86
Full Bombarde Organ with Ophicleide	88 8888 888	88

THE PEDAL SOLO UNIT

The Pedal Solo Unit gives the more ambitious church or concert organist a magnificent and adequate foundation of bass upon which to build the tone of his ensemble. The pedal tone of the oldest of musical instruments has been through the centuries the foundation of manual tone. The latter lacks the majesty and power of large pedal pipes, sometimes 37 feet in length and 3 feet in diameter. Together, a complete complement of tone exists. The Hammond Pedal Solo Unit, when played through a sufficient number of speakers, produces a rich and deep bass to balance a Diapason Chorus combined with a Reed Chorus. Its effect, remembering that *all* musical effects are *absolutely* dependent upon acoustical environment, is worthy of sincere praise.

Flexible and rapid passages for the feet usually are without benefit of the deep 32' stops. On this new Unit, tones usually requiring three seconds to generate from pipes as tall as a house are produced instantaneously. This is a benefit of electronic tone generation. Also, when the organist lifts his foot from depressing the very deep tones, they cease to speak instantaneously. If the tones had come from really large pipes, the sound wave would have taken three seconds after the pedal-key release to stop generating.

The effect of the Pedal Solo Unit can be had with soft playing, too. An inaudible (but present) bass for a String Organ can be subconscious or conscious in its effect on listeners. Any 32'-stop tone can be reduced in volume to any degree of softness required by the volume knob. Thus, a living-room or a great concert auditorium can be served by these 32'-stop tones.

In addition to the 32' stops, the Pedal Solo Unit contains stops of 16', 8', 4', 2', and 1' pitches. Concert organists, proud of their foot technique, need high-pitched stops to be heard in very rapid passages. Well-practiced heel and toe have a way of adding much to good hand manipulation.

Stop controls, containing fundamentals and overtones, of the following designations are provided in the Pedal Unit:

2' and 1'
4'
8'
16'
32' Bourdon (basic tone)
32' Bombarde (reed tone)

Those besides the 32' stops have no names attached, but are useful with any tone qualities. Several of these stops can be drawn simultaneously to make a composite tone. The standard pedal Harmonic Controllers, present with or without the Pedal Solo Unit, can be used at the same time as the Pedal Solo Unit. It serves to brighten the pedal tone. (One of the Solo Unit's unique features is that it is completely separate from the manuals, and generates its own tones independently.)

If two pedal keys are depressed when the Pedal Solo Unit is turned on, only the higher one plays. This permits the less-bright standard Harmonic Controllers to furnish an accompaniment by the left foot for the Solo Unit (and Harmonic Controllers also) from the right foot.

Usually 16' and 18' stops provide enough bass for average use. 32' stops should be used sparingly. They are intended to support a considerable mass of tone, and their effect can be quickly monotonous and cloying to the senses. Because of their profundity they provide a contrast to the ordinary bass, but their effect is lost by too frequent use. They parallel brilliant and intense hues; they have a purpose, as does scarlet or purple in painting. *Use them sparingly* is a good motto for all organists. Their lower pitches are indefinite; they are in existence because of their great array of overtones.

The 32' Bourdon is sometimes pleasant in "heavier" hymn singing, while the 32' Bombarde can be useful only to balance great manual power.

The stop control marked "Mute" softens the higher-pitched Solo Unit stops. An "Off-On" switch controls the Unit's entire group of stops.

The average player who has not had organ instruction will be confronted by the problem of whether or not to attempt to use the Pedal keyboard. The answer to this question will eventually be yes. No one would be permanently satisfied to let the world of the Pedal Organ go unexplored. It contains too many desirable effects, and too much power that can be added to the Full Organ, to neglect because of the effort required to place one's foot on a few broad keys.

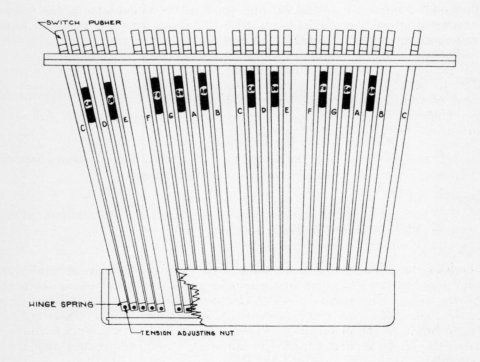

Figure 5

The Pedal Keyboard

PLAYING THE PEDAL KEYBOARD

A half-hour a day for one month is enough to master to an average degree the problems of the Pedal keyboard.

Below is presented a series of suggestions to be worked out by every reader in his own time and in his own way. When they have been followed, the player will be able to say, "I play with my feet, too." There is no substitute for regular lessons, and the player should take such lessons if he has the inclination. But if time or other interests do not permit this, and the player wishes to increase the satisfaction obtained from his pipe-organ, the following exercises will prove useful:

Exercise No. 1:

Sit in front of the center of the organ. *Sit up straight.* Look at the Pedal keyboard. Place the left foot (toe) between the lowest E♭ and F♯. This is a "toe-space". Now place the left foot between the lowest B♭ and the C♯ beside it. This is also a "toe-space". Look at the music-rack and place the left foot in these two toe-spaces alternately. This must be done by feeling the black Pedal-keys. Leave the console. Come back and place the left foot in these two toe-spaces without looking at the feet.

Exercise No. 2:

From these two toe-spaces, find each white Pedal-key in the lowest octave of the Pedal keyboard. Play the scale with the left foot alone beginning on the lowest C. Use heel and toe alternately, beginning with the toe.

Exercise No. 3:

Play the bass parts to the following hymns, while the hands play at the same time:
1. "Sun Of My Soul"
2. "My Faith Looks Up To Thee"

Use the left foot alone, the first time. If a long "jump" occurs between notes, try to use the right foot for the higher note.

Exercise No. 4:

Try to play harder hymns of your own selection. Never look at the feet unless you are hopelessly lost.

Exercise No. 5:

Select some piece of music of the degree of difficulty of Schubert's "Serenade". With the feet play the notes that you believe to be the important bass notes.

Exercise No. 6:

Select a fairly difficult piece of piano music and mark with circles the notes you intend to use for the feet. Play the selection.

Exercise No. 7:

Purchase, if you desire, some easy organ music, with a third staff for the feet. Practise the Pedal parts alone first. Then join hands and feet.

Exercise No. 8:

Sit at the console looking at the music-rack. Think of some note on the Pedal keyboard which you desire to find quickly. Attempt to set the foot down on it without using the black keys along the toe-spaces to feel its position. Do not confine your efforts to the lower octave of the Pedal keyboard.

Review every previous lesson for the first eight minutes of each lesson period. Never become discouraged; you are learning to control your feet in a much shorter time than you learned to control your hands.

THE ACCOMPANIMENT OF VOICES

The accompaniment of voices, whether in groups or singly, demands special care in the selection of the stops to be used. The Diapasons have for years been the standard tone for accompanying hymn-singing in churches. The tone of the Diapason is neither so brilliant as to detract from the timbre of the voice nor too dull to give support to it.

The Diapason is, however, best suited to the accompaniment of groups of singers. The Flute is valuable in accompanying single voices, particularly women's voices; but the best timbre possible for accompanying a single voice is something between a Flute and a Diapason. This need not necessarily be a perfect hybrid stop.

Here are three series of number-arrangements for accompanying voices. The use of the Expression Pedal will make it possible to adjust the volume to exactly the right amount.

Single Voice	Small Group	Large Group
00 4210 000	00 5320 000	00 6654 000
00 6421 000	00 6543 100	00 6665 200
00 7532 000	00 6543 200	00 6665 300
00 7632 000	00 6544 300	00 7765 300
00 7633 000	00 6544 310	00 7765 310
00 7643 000	00 6544 320	00 7765 210
00 7654 000	00 6554 100	00 7765 320
00 7665 000	00 6554 200	00 7765 321
00 8765 000	00 6554 300	00 8876 320
00 8766 100	00 6554 321	00 8875 432
00 8766 210	00 7654 310	00 8887 321
00 8766 310	00 7865 320	00 8878 231
00 8776 310	00 8776 430	00 8878 430
00 8776 320	00 8765 540	00 8878 431
00 8854 100	00 8764 321	00 8878 532
00 8873 100	00 8765 321	00 8888 730
00 8875 000	00 8555 543	00 8888 850

If the organist must accompany several hundred or even several thousand voices, a Reed tone (which also includes Diapason tone) is the most valuable. Be careful not to draw the three highest Harmonic Controllers in excess of a hybrid between a Diapason and a Reed. Here are some examples of moderately developed accompanimental tones:

```
00 8876 210
00 8876 310
00 8876 410
00 8876 510
00 8876 320
00 8876 430
00 8876 530
00 8876 540
00 8876 650
00 8876 510
00 8876 610
```

Following are examples of combinations to be used for accompanying very large audiences or congregations; these examples are distinctly brass-like in tone. Like the former set, they include Diapason tone in their timbre.

```
00 7777 540
01 7777 540
10 7777 540
20 7777 540
30 7777 540
20 7777 541
30 7777 541
10 8887 541
20 8887 541
30 8887 541
40 8887 541
41 8887 541
12 8887 653
21 8888 651
12 8888 651
23 8888 651
32 8888 653
55 8888 765
84 8888 873
85 8888 873
63 8888 874
63 8888 875
63 8888 876
84 8888 876
74 8888 876
73 8888 876
75 8888 876
```

THE ORGAN WITH ORCHESTRA OR BAND

Every organist will some time find it necessary to play with an orchestra or band. The organ in such cases is usually desired because of its wonderful supporting qualities or heavy bass tones. The organ makes a perfect complement to any musical organization. An orchestra may lack one particular instrument, such as a Trumpet or a French Horn; the organ can always play the part of that missing instrument.

Another valuable addition to the orchestra is a sustained background of high-pitched chords played on such a stop as 00 5665 321 or 00 8653 100. If the middle registers of the orchestra are lacking, Diapasons are the most desirable stops to use. A Diapason-orchestral combination is 10 8765 310.

If great power is desired to support the orchestra or band, and the music is of a loud nature, 31 8888 850 is a desirable stop to use.

If an organ concerto is to be played, the organist must study the score with the idea of selecting the appropriate stops, of either orchestral or organ type, to suit the concerto in question.

Frequently a contest between the organ and the orchestra is used as a novelty number. Here the organist could rely on 74 8888 886.

Another possibility for using the organ with band or orchestra is in outdoor playing. When playing outdoors, the organist should seldom use any of the three Harmonic Controllers at the right. A desirable outdoor combination is 00 8853 000.

The speaker of the organ should be near the orchestra or band when accompanimental work is done. The source of sound of the organ should seem to the listeners identical with the position of the orchestra or band.

To accompany Chimes, either in the organ or at another source, the organist will find 00 6410 000 or 00 3210 000 useful. The higher harmonics of the organ would, if used with the Chimes, obscure their delicate timbre.

When used with a dance orchestra, the organ can take solo parts or accompanimental parts. Novelty numbers are frequently heard with the organ's great resources used to good advantage. Three instruments and an organ make an orchestra large enough for many purposes, and two organs with an orchestra make a very interesting combination. Trick stops of the weirder sort or the standard organ tones can be used.

There is a growing interest in organ music. Radio concerts on the organ are increasingly popular. The combination of organ and orchestra is bound to become more appreciated as it is heard more often. More powerful effects are possible, and more variety is obtained, when these two are played together.

In playing with an orchestra or band, the organist should always follow the conductor. To the conductor the organ is simply one of his instruments, and he is responsible for the effect of the whole organization.

One prominent orchestra conductor has conceived the idea of making up an "orchestra" of four or more organs. One organ would play the part of the Strings, one would play the Brass parts, one would play the Wood-wind parts, and one would play the important bass parts.

ACOUSTICS AND THE ORGAN

There are many sizes, shapes, and types of rooms in which the organ must speak. The tones of the organ, like all musical tones, are immensely affected by the dimensions, furnishings, and wall-treatment of the room. The same organ will sound different in different rooms. The organist can use the same stops, volume, and selection; but there will be a difference in the effect on the listener. The study of these differences belongs to the science of acoustics.

It is even possible to make the same organ sound different by placing it in different positions in the same room. A study of each room is therefore necessary to determine which position for the speaker of the organ is best for the listener.

Problems in acoustics have been a trial for architects even from ancient times. The early cathedral builders frequently had the problem of an echo to solve. Lacking corrective tiles and plasters, they had to put up with the undesirable sound-reflections or rebuild. Today it is usually possible to correct any acoustical difficulty in a theater, cathedral, or auditorium after it has been built.

The great orchestral conductors and singers are so sensitive to acoustic conditions that they frequently become very particular where they play or sing. The subject of acoustics is important to the musician who wants to obtain the maximum from his performance.

The chief problem in acoustics is to find the "happy medium" between too much and too little reflection from the walls, ceiling, and floor. After a sound wave has been generated within the limits of an enclosure, it does not cease to jump between walls, ceiling, and floor when its source stops vibrating. A certain amount of reverberation is heard afterwards. The length of time that this reverberation continues is called the "reverberation time". To adjust this reverberation time is a problem for the acoustic engineer.

The reverberation time in the various places where organs are required to play varies to a tremendous extent. In a high, bare-walled cathedral the reverberation may continue for as long as fifteen seconds. In an over-furnished funeral parlor the reverberation may seem to cease instantly when the sound-source stops vibrating. These present the two extremes in acoustical problems.

Hard walls permit the sound waves to spring elastically back and forth between their confines several times before the energy is dissipated. Rooms fitted with heavy rugs and curtains readily absorb the energy of the sound waves. The higher harmonics are more quickly absorbed and easily lost than the lower ones.

The best length of time for reverberation to continue after a sound has been made has been a subject of discussion. It has been suggested that an auditorium have four seconds. Many musicians want a shorter reverberation period. Standards in this field are usually personal, and every musician tries to maintain the particular conditions he feels are best for his temperament.

Great satisfaction is obtained from the music of an organ which has been installed with careful regard to acoustics. In such a room soft music is amplified; loud music is allowed to spread in such a way that it is not too intense to the listener's ear.

Consideration of a few fundamental problems in furnishing the room and in selecting the position for the organ speaker will yield musical satisfaction not obtainable in any other way. Correct acoustics cannot be simulated. Sacrifices may have to be made in furnishings, or a little expense may result from changes; but to the lover of music the result is worth almost any effort.

Many homes and small churches have too short a reverberation time. It is possible to correct this trouble in most cases. A good rule is: the smaller the room, the more bare surfaces there should be; the larger the room, the more covered surfaces are needed. The person testing a room for its acoustic qualities may proceed in many different ways. The most common way is to clap the hands sharply in the room at the exact position the organ speaker is intended to occupy. If the reverberation of the sound thus generated continues for one, two, three, or four seconds, no further treatment of the room is necessary in installing the organ. If, however, the reverberation time is shorter, some furnishings of the type of velvet curtains, or other soft, porous material should be removed. Frequently, substituting several small rugs for one large rug is desirable. If the reverberation time exceeds four seconds, a competent acoustic engineer should be consulted.

The placing of the speaker can also materially contribute to the success of an organ installation. There are two rules which should always be followed:

1. Place the speaker in a position which causes the sound coming from the cones to strike some object like a wall, floor, ceiling, or reflecting screen *before* it reaches the ears of the listener. The sound must never reach the listener until it has been reflected at least once;

2. Place the speaker in a position which will permit it to be near the greatest amount of bare reflecting surface.

In home installations, one of the best places for the speaker is in the ceiling of a two- or three-story stair-well. The console should be below, in the living room. The sound waves will have been reflected several times when they reach the ears of the organist and the listeners. A bare closet near the top of the stair-well is an almost equally desirable place for the speaker. It should be completely emptied, and a damask or organ-pipe screen substituted for the door.

There are many possibilities for unique installations in homes. The largest room in the house is usually the best one acoustically.

Three phases of organ-playing are particularly affected by acoustic conditions:

1. The use of the Tremulant
2. Playing bass notes
3. Drawing the highest Harmonic Controllers

In a small room the Tremulant is more noticeable than in a large room. In a large auditorium the Tremulant is sometimes concealed by the reverberations. Let the amount of tremolo used be in proportion to the size of the room.

Large rooms can absorb easily the powerful, slow vibrations of bass notes. The proportion of pedal volume to manual volume should be greater in a large room and smaller in a small room. In determining the right degree of bass volume on the Pedal Organ, one of the most helpful things an organist can do is to have someone else take the console for a few minutes while he makes a trip around the whole room, listening at every point to the bass. At a distance from the organ speaker the bass seems louder in proportion to the higher notes than close to the speaker. There is a certain proportion above which the bass should not speak louder than the treble. This proportion, between bass and treble, sounds different to different listeners. Some ears are offended by even a little bass; others need it to gain what they refer to as a "well-rounded" tone. Bass vibrations are usually very intense in proportion to their frequency. They fatigue quickly, just as very high notes do.

If a sharp Trumpet stop is played in a well-curtained room which is full of people, it has somewhat the quality of a String tone. If a keen 'Cello stop is played in a larger room, it has somewhat the quality of a Reed tone. Therefore, adjustment of the Harmonic Controllers to the size and nature of the room is necessary. Flutes, having fewer harmonics than the other divisions of tone, do not need adjustment of this type. It is necessary to make the number-arrangements more brilliant for larger rooms and less brilliant for smaller rooms in order to gain the best effect.

The acoustic characteristics of a room affect greatly the success or failure of the music performed in it. The study of acoustics deserves all the attention a musician can give to it.

A Reverberation Unit has been developed which adapts the Hammond Organ to a great variety of smaller rooms which do not have enough reverberation time before the sound waves cease to exist. Part of the electricity going from the console to the speakers is diverted through a circuit traveling through five long coiled springs immersed in tubes of oil. It naturally takes the electricity longer to travel through the springs, which move up and down, delaying the sound's ceasing (by continuing the circuit) than to flow directly into the speakers. This delayed ceasing of the sound in a small amount of power used in the organ quite perfectly simulates the reflection and continued re-reflection between walls and ceiling and floor.

MAIN TONE GENERATOR

Each Hammond Organ console has a complement of ninety-one individual tone-generating units. These units produce all the pitches of tones available on the organ. Let us inquire a little into some technical detail in this brand new principle of generating a true musical tone.

More than five hundred different shapes and forms of organ pipes exist in pipe-organs. Each shape of pipe makes its own tone quality or timbre produced by a fundamental tone (the basic one or lowest in pitch) and a complicated series of varying strengths of overtones which we hear at the same time, but do not recognize as different in pitch from the fundamental or unison pitch. The fundamental and overtones both must always be analyzed in every musical tone synthesis. Overtones exist for the simple reason that a long steel rod would not vibrate, in fact could not vibrate, as one bowed segment; the small segments each bowing along with the longest make their own individual tones or pitches, usually weaker than the fundamental or longest segment. These small segments exist in air columns vibrating as both open or stopped pipes. These segments correspond to overtones. They lend individuality to tone.

The Hammond Organ must generate both fundamental and many overtones at the same time.   Each of these, of course, bears a different pitch for us to hear simultaneously.   Our brain reflexes analyze the presence and strengths of overtones to tell us whether a Violin or a Flute is playing the same pitch and volume when we cannot see the instruments.   In the console a series of ninety-one wheels made of steel, and about two inches in diameter, rotate all of the time the organ is turned on.   As vibrations must come with regularity, they must be made to turn accurately at a definite velocity.   Many of them play when one key is depressed.   Each one produces a single pitch.

On the circumference of each wheel is a series of serrations, "hills and valleys", which pass in the presence of a small electromagnet a few inches long.   These serrations disturb the field around the electromagnet just as many times per second as the pitch requires.   The disturbances travel along the wire connected to the electromagnet and finally become, after a complicated circuiting through tubes and amplifiers, a sound wave from a speaker cone.   Millions of amplifications are necessary, as the tiny magnet can produce only a little energy, and a great deal is needed to move the tons of air in a large church, or the hundreds of pounds in a living room.   Moving this air is necessary to actuate the ears.

A limb waving in the wind or a pair of lips against a tube naturally vibrate at the same time in both the fundamental and overtones.   However, in the Hammond Organ we must have simulated in a systematic way each tone if we are to achieve an effect, for example, of a Flute.

The ninety-one tone wheels give us these ground-tones or basic tones with which to work.   With modern electrical machinery we can vary the basic vibrations in intensity (volume), in pitch (frequency), produce *céleste*-like undulations as of many instruments playing at the same time, and make tremolos of any speed or degree.

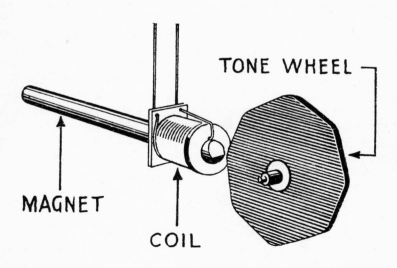

Figure 6

Tone Generator

THE HAMMOND SPINET

A recent, smaller model of the Hammond Organ adapted for simplified use is the Spinet. It has all of the essential tonal features of the larger Hammond models but has been especially devised for use in smaller enclosures. It can be clearly heard in a room seating up to one hundred people.

Probably the feature to be noticed first is the placing of the speaker in the console unit. This simplifies problems of moving, and provides ample volume for average size enclosures. In most churches a speaker system larger than the Spinet would be required, but for the small church seating up to about one hundred people, providing the church is acoustically "live", the Spinet is adequate.

Another feature is the shortened upper and lower manuals. The lower manual, usually accompanimental to the upper manual, has 44 keys, and extends farther below middle-C than the upper. The upper manual, usually for right-hand and melody or solo playing, also has 44 keys, and extends farther above middle-C than the lower. The lower manual may well be used to accompany hymns, both hands playing on it together, as it has more keys for bass parts (which are duplicated on the Pedal keyboard), and also a more brilliant set of Harmonic Controllers. These two new overtones, the 10th and the 12th, are not available on the upper keyboard.

The Pedal keyboard possesses twelve keys, including all the sharps and flats in one complete octave, and is readily played by any pianist with practically no preliminary practice.

A single draw-bar (Harmonic Controller) is provided for the pedal tone. Stop controls for normal or slow pedal attack and normal or fast pedal delay are provided. The Spinet swell pedal incorporates an automatic legato device specifically designed to assist the beginner in getting familiar with the Pedal keyboard.

The Spinet model also has stop controls for vibrato, and a *céleste*-like vibrato chorus. These are much the same as on the larger models. On the newest models of the Spinet a Selective Vibrato system has been added. This permits the organist to achieve a vibrato effect from either or both of the manuals. A Violin solo, for example, may be played with vibrato on the upper manual, accompanied by a non-vibrato String and Flute combination on the lower manual. Electrical connections for a phonograph, radio, or microphone are provided. The organ can be played at the same time these connections are being used.

Although the Spinet has simplified tone controls, the famous flexibility of voicing stops right at the console has been retained in this model, as in all models of Hammond consoles.

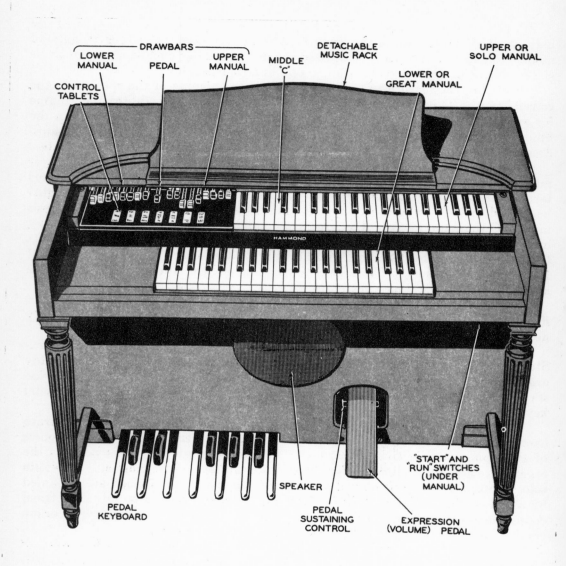

Figure 7

The Hammond Spinet

THE DICTIONARY

THE FOUNDATION STOPS

Accompanimental Diapason 8'
No. 1....................02 8844 321
No. 2....................01 7722 100
No. 3....................00 8875 321
No. 4....................00 8874 210
No. 5....................00 8873 210
No. 6....................00 8872 210
No. 7....................00 8871 100
No. 8....................00 8865 321
No. 9....................00 8864 210
No. 10....................00 8863 210
No. 11....................00 8862 200
No. 12....................00 8861 100
No. 13....................00 8854 210
No. 14....................00 8853 210
No. 15....................00 8852 200
No. 16....................00 8851 100
No. 17....................00 8843 321
No. 18....................00 8842 210
No. 19....................00 8841 210
No. 20....................00 8832 210
No. 21....................00 8831 200
No. 22....................00 8821 100
No. 23....................00 7764 210
No. 24....................00 7763 210
No. 25....................00 7762 200
No. 26....................00 7761 100
No. 27....................00 7753 100
No. 28....................00 7752 100
No. 29....................00 7751 000
No. 30....................00 7743 210
No. 31....................00 7742 200
No. 32....................00 7741 100
No. 33....................00 7732 100
No. 34....................00 7731 100
No. 35....................00 7721 100
No. 36....................00 6654 321
No. 37....................00 6653 210
No. 38....................00 6652 100
No. 39....................00 6651 100

Aequalprinzipal 8'
No. 1....................00 8824 100
No. 2....................00 8824 000

Bass Open Diapason 16'
No. 1....................85 8532 000
No. 2....................85 8531 000

Bell Diapason 8'
No. 1....................00 8856 540
No. 2....................00 8856 530
No. 3....................00 8856 520
No. 4....................00 8856 510
No. 5....................00 8856 500
No. 6....................00 8856 430
No. 7....................00 8856 420
No. 8....................00 8856 410
No. 9....................00 8856 400
No. 10....................00 8856 320
No. 11....................00 8856 310
No. 12....................00 8856 300
No. 13....................00 8856 210
No. 14....................00 8856 200
No. 15....................00 8856 100

Campana 1'
....................00 0000 006

Cathedral Diapason 8'
No. 1....................00 7755 430
No. 2....................00 7755 420
No. 3....................00 7755 410
No. 4....................00 7755 400
No. 5....................00 7755 320
No. 6....................00 7755 310
No. 7....................00 7755 300
No. 8....................00 7755 210
No. 9....................00 7755 200
No. 10....................00 7755 100
No. 11....................00 7755 000

Choir Diapason 8'
No. 1....................00 7744 321
No. 2....................00 7744 311
No. 3....................00 7744 301
No. 4....................00 7744 211
No. 5....................00 7744 201
No. 6....................00 7744 101
No. 7....................00 7744 001

Choralbasset 2′	00	0008 003
Chorus Diapason 16′	84	8421 000

Chorus Diapason 8′

No. 1	00	8686 321
No. 2	00	8686 320
No. 3	00	8686 310
No. 4	00	8686 210
No. 5	00	8686 100
Chorus Diapason 4′	00	0806 086
Contra Cathedral Diapason 16′	75	7510 000

Contra Diapason 16′

No. 1	85	8521 000
No. 2	85	8520 000
Contra Geigen Diapason 16′	88	6732 000
Contra Open Diapason 16′	85	8521 000
Contra Prinzipal 16′	87	8621 000

Contra Solo Diapason 16′

No. 1	85	8544 000
No. 2	85	8533 000

Diapason 16′	75	8632 100

Diapason 8′

No. 1	00	7785 421
No. 2	00	7785 420
No. 3	00	7785 321
No. 4	00	7785 210
No. 5	00	7785 110
No. 6	00	7783 421
No. 7	00	7783 420
No. 8	00	7783 321
No. 9	00	7783 210
No. 10	00	7783 110
Diapason 4′	00	0707 082

Diapason Chorus

No. 1	82	8855 442
No. 2	82	8855 441
No. 3	82	8855 440
No. 4	82	8855 432
No. 5	82	8855 431
No. 6	82	8855 430
No. 7	82	8855 421
No. 8	82	8855 420
No. 9	82	8855 410
No. 10	82	8855 326
No. 11	82	8855 325
No. 12	82	8855 324
No. 13	82	8855 323
No. 14	82	8855 212
No. 15	61	8855 543
No. 16	61	8855 542
No. 17	61	8855 541
No. 18	61	8855 424
No. 19	61	8855 423
No. 20	61	8855 422

Diapason Chorus and Mixtures

No. 1	84	8855 556
No. 2	83	8855 445
No. 3	83	8855 332

Diapason Fifteenth 2′	00	0006 005

Diapason Magna 8′

No. 1	02	8866 542
No. 2	02	8866 541
No. 3	02	8866 540
No. 4	02	8866 531
No. 5	02	8866 530
No. 6	02	8866 520
No. 7	02	8866 510
No. 8	02	8866 500
No. 9	02	8866 431
No. 10	02	8866 430
No. 11	02	8866 420
No. 12	02	8866 410
No. 13	02	8866 400
No. 14	02	8866 320
No. 15	02	8866 310
No. 16	02	8866 300
No. 17	02	8866 210
No. 18	02	8866 200
No. 19	02	8866 100

Diapason Nineteenth 1⅓′	00	0000 060
Diapason Octave Quint 2⅔′	00	0060 000

Diapason Phonon 8′

No. 1	00	8877 651
No. 2	00	8877 650
No. 3	00	8877 641
No. 4	00	8877 640

Diapason Phonon 8′

No. 5	00 8877 630
No. 6	00 8877 620
No. 7	00 8877 610
No. 8	00 8877 600
No. 9	00 8877 540
No. 10	00 8877 530
No. 11	00 8877 520
No. 12	00 8877 510
No. 13	00 8877 500
No. 14	00 8877 430
No. 15	00 8877 420
No. 16	00 8877 410
No. 17	00 8877 400
No. 18	00 8877 320
No. 19	00 9877 310
No. 20	00 8877 300
No. 21	00 8877 210
No. 22	00 8877 200
No. 23	00 8877 100
No. 24	00 8877 000

Diapason Profunda 16′

No. 1	86 8644 210
No. 2	86 8644 200

Diapason Quint 5⅓′   06 0010 000
Diapason Seventeenth 1⅓′   00 0000 060
Diapason Sonora 8′

No. 1	01 8844 331
No. 2	01 8844 330
No. 3	01 8844 321
No. 4	01 8844 320
No. 5	01 8844 310
No. 6	01 8844 300
No. 7	01 8844 221
No. 8	01 8844 220
No. 9	01 8844 210
No. 10	01 8844 200
No. 11	01 8844 110
No. 12	01 8844 100
No. 13	01 8844 000

Diapason Twelfth 2⅔′   00 0060 010
Diapason Twenty-second 1′   00 0000 006

Double Diapason 16′

No. 1	74 7432 100
No. 2	74 7432 000
No. 3	74 7431 000
No. 4	74 7421 000
No. 5	74 7420 000

Doublette 2′   00 0006 000
Double Viola Diapason 16′   75 7543 100
Double Violin Diapason 16′

No. 1	75 7544 210
No. 2	75 7533 210

Echo Diapason 16′

No. 1	43 4421 000
No. 2	43 4420 000

Echo Diapason 8′

No. 1	00 4434 210
No. 2	00 4434 110
No. 3	00 4434 100

Echo Diapason 4′   00 0404 034
English Diapason 16′   62 6210 000
English Diapason 8′

No. 1	00 6634 211
No. 2	00 6634 210

English Diapason 4′   00 0606 034

Fifteenth 2′

No. 1	00 0006 000
No. 2	00 0005 001

Flue Twelfth 2⅔′   00 0060 010
Flute à Pavillon 8′

No. 1	00 8856 540
No. 2	00 8856 530
No. 3	00 8856 520
No. 4	00 8856 510
No. 5	00 8856 500
No. 6	00 8856 430
No. 7	00 8856 420
No. 8	00 8856 410
No. 9	00 8856 400
No. 10	00 8856 320
No. 11	00 8856 310
No. 12	00 8856 300
No. 13	00 8856 210
No. 14	00 8856 200
No. 15	00 8856 100

Geigen Diapason 16′   88 6732 100
Geigen Diapason 8′

No. 1	00 8687 431
No. 2	00 8687 430
No. 3	00 8687 421
No. 4	00 8687 420

Geigen Diapason 4'........00 0806 087
Geigen Octave 4'..........00 0806 087
Gothic Diapason 8'
  No. 1...................00 6766 433
  No. 2...................00 6766 432
  No. 3...................00 6766 431
  No. 4...................00 6766 430
  No. 5...................00 6766 323
  No. 6...................00 6766 322
  No. 7...................00 6766 321
  No. 8...................00 6766 320
  No. 9...................00 6766 212
  No. 10..................00 6766 210
  No. 11..................00 6766 110
  No. 12..................00 6766 100
Grand Diapason 16'
  No. 1...................86 8642 000
  No. 2...................86 8641 000
  No. 3...................86 8640 000
  No. 4...................86 8632 000
  No. 5...................86 8631 000
  No. 6...................86 8630 000
  No. 7...................86 8621 000
  No. 8...................86 8620 000
  No. 9...................86 8610 000

Grand Diapason 8'
  No. 1 ....00 8866 540
  No. 2...................00 8866 530
  No. 3...................00 8866 520
  No. 4...................00 8866 510
  No. 5...................00 8866 500
  No. 6...................00 8866 430
  No. 7...................00 8866 420
  No. 8...................00 8866 410
  No. 9...................00 8866 400
  No. 10..................00 8866 320
  No. 11..................00 8866 310
  No. 12..................00 8866 300
  No. 13..................00 8866 210
  No. 14..................00 8866 200
  No. 15..................00 8866 100
  No. 16..................00 8866 000

Grand Diapason Chorus
  No. 1...................86 8877 543
  No. 2...................86 8877 542
  No. 3...................86 8877 545
Grand Prinzipal 8'
  No. 1...................01 8855 430
  No. 2...................01 8855 420
  No. 3...................01 8855 410
  No. 4...................01 8855 400
  No. 5...................01 8855 320
  No. 6...................01 8855 310
  No. 7...................01 8855 300
  No. 8...................01 8855 210
  No. 9...................01 8855 200
  No. 10..................01 8855 100
  No. 11..................01 8855 000
Gross Diapason 16'........85 8522 100

Harmonic Diapason 16'
  No. 1...................85 8524 100
  No. 2...................85 8523 100

Harmonic Diapason 8'
  No. 1...................00 8877 760
  No. 2...................00 8877 750
  No. 3...................00 8877 740
  No. 4...................00 8877 730
  No. 5...................00 8877 720
  No. 6...................00 8877 710
  No. 7...................00 8877 700
  No. 8...................00 8866 650
  No. 9...................00 8866 640
  No. 10..................00 8866 630
  No. 11..................00 8866 620
  No. 12..................00 8866 610
  No. 13..................00 8866 600
  No. 14..................00 8855 540
  No. 15..................00 8855 530
  No. 16..................00 8855 520
  No. 17..................00 8855 510
  No. 18..................00 8855 500
  No. 19..................00 8844 430
  No. 20..................00 8844 420
  No. 21..................00 8844 410
  No. 22..................00 8844 400
  No. 23..................00 8678 452
  No. 24..................00 8678 451
  No. 25..................00 8678 453
  No. 26..................00 8678 344
  No. 27..................00 8678 342
  No. 28..................00 8678 322
  No. 29..................00 7766 650
  No. 30..................00 7766 640
  No. 31..................00 7766 630
  No. 32..................00 7766 620
  No. 33..................00 7766 610
  No. 34..................00 7766 600

Harmonic Diapason 8'

No. 35	00 7755 540
No. 36	00 7755 530
No. 37	00 7755 520
No. 38	00 7755 510
No. 39	00 7755 500
No. 40	00 7744 430
No. 41	00 7744 420
No. 42	00 7744 410
No. 43	00 7744 400
No. 44	00 8657 453
No. 45	00 8657 452
No. 46	00 8657 455
No. 47	00 8657 343
No. 48	00 8657 344
No. 49	00 8657 231
No. 50	00 6655 540
No. 51	00 6655 530
No. 52	00 6655 520
No. 53	00 6655 510
No. 54	00 6655 500
No. 55	00 6644 430
No. 56	00 6644 420
No. 57	00 6644 410
No. 58	00 6644 400
No. 59	00 6556 432
No. 60	00 6556 431
No. 61	00 6556 430
No. 62	00 6556 342
No. 63	00 6556 344
No. 64	00 6556 456
No. 65	00 5544 430
No. 66	00 5544 420
No. 67	00 5544 410
No. 68	00 5544 400
No. 69	00 6546 532
No. 70	00 6546 531
No. 71	00 6546 530
No. 72	00 6546 521
No. 73	00 6546 520
No. 74	00 6546 510
No. 75	00 6546 511
No. 76	00 6546 512
No. 77	00 6546 422
No. 78	00 6546 414
No. 79	00 6546 415
No. 80	00 6546 413
No. 81	00 6546 412
No. 82	00 6546 411
No. 83	00 6546 410
No. 84	00 6546 323

Harmonic Diapason 4'

No. 1	00 0606 045
No. 2	00 0505 034
No. 3	00 0404 023

Horn Diapason 16'

No. 1	88 8621 000
No. 2	77 7621 000
No. 3	66 6421 000

Horn Diapason 8'

No. 1	00 8887 650
No. 2	00 8887 640
No. 3	00 8887 630
No. 4	00 8887 620
No. 5	00 8887 610
No. 6	00 8887 600
No. 7	00 8887 540
No. 8	00 8887 530
No. 9	00 8887 520
No. 10	00 8887 510

Horn Diapason 8′

No. 11	00 8887 500
No. 12	00 8887 430
No. 13	00 8887 420
No. 14	00 8887 410
No. 15	00 8887 400
No. 16	00 8887 320
No. 17	00 8887 310
No. 18	00 8887 300
No. 19	00 8887 210
No. 20	00 8887 200
No. 21	00 8887 100
No. 22	00 8887 000
No. 23	00 8886 540
No. 24	00 8886 530
No. 25	00 8886 520
No. 26	00 8886 510
No. 27	00 8886 500
No. 28	00 8886 430
No. 29	00 8886 420
No. 30	00 8886 410
No. 31	00 8886 400
No. 32	00 8886 320
No. 33	00 8886 310
No. 34	00 8886 300
No. 35	00 8886 210
No. 36	00 8886 200
No. 37	00 8886 100
No. 38	00 8886 000
No. 39	00 8886 010
No. 40	00 8885 430
No. 41	00 8885 420
No. 42	00 8885 410
No. 43	00 8885 400
No. 44	00 8885 320
No. 45	00 8885 310
No. 46	00 8885 300
No. 47	00 8885 210
No. 48	00 8885 200
No. 49	00 8885 100
No. 50	00 8885 000
No. 51	00 8884 320
No. 52	00 8884 310
No. 53	00 8884 300
No. 54	00 8884 210
No. 55	00 8884 200
No. 56	00 8884 100
No. 57	00 8884 000
No. 58	00 8748 321
No. 59	00 8748 320
No. 60	00 8748 311
No. 61	00 8748 310
No. 62	00 8748 211
No. 63	00 8748 210
No. 64	00 8748 212
No. 65	00 7776 540
No. 66	00 7776 530

Horn Diapason 8′

No. 67	00 7776 520
No. 68	00 7776 510
No. 69	00 7776 500
No. 70	00 7776 430
No. 71	00 7776 420
No. 72	00 7776 410
No. 73	00 7776 400
No. 74	00 7776 320
No. 75	00 7776 310
No. 76	00 7776 300
No. 77	00 7776 210
No. 78	00 7776 200
No. 79	00 7776 100
No. 80	00 7776 000
No. 81	00 7775 430
No. 82	00 7775 420
No. 83	00 7775 410
No. 84	00 7775 400
No. 85	00 7775 320
No. 86	00 7775 310
No. 87	00 7775 300
No. 88	00 7775 210
No. 89	00 7775 200
No. 90	00 7775 100
No. 91	00 7775 000
No. 92	00 7774 320
No. 93	00 7774 310
No. 94	00 7774 300
No 95	00 7774 210
No. 96	00 7774 200
No. 97	00 7774 100
No. 98	00 7774 000

Horn Diapason 4′
No. 1. .00 0606 063
No. 2. .00 0505 052

Kleinprinzipal 4′. 00 0704 020

Larigot 1⅓′. 00 0000 060

Major Diapason 16′. 87 8743 000
Major Diapason 8′
No. 1. .02 8877 651
No. 2. .02 8877 650
No. 3. .02 8877 640
No. 4. .02 8877 630
No. 5. .02 8877 620
No. 6. .02 8877 610
No. 7. .02 8877 600
No. 8. .02 8877 540
No. 9. .02 8877 530
No. 10. . . . . .02 8877 520
No. 11. . . . . .02 8877 510
No. 12. . . . . .02 8877 500
No. 13. . . . . .02 8877 430
No. 14. . . . . .02 8877 420
No. 15. . . . . .02 8877 410
No. 16. . . . . .02 8877 400
No. 17. . . . . .02 8877 320
No. 18. . . . . .02 8877 310
No. 19. . . . . .02 8877 300
No. 20. . . . . .02 8877 210
No. 21. . . . . .02 8877 200
No. 22. . . . . .02 8877 100
No. 23. . . . . .02 8877 000
Minor Diapason 8′
No. 1. .00 7766 540
No. 2. .00 7766 530
No. 3. .00 7766 520
No. 4. .00 7766 510
No. 5. .00 7766 500
No. 6. .00 7766 430
No. 7. .00 7766 420
No. 8. .00 7766 410
No. 9. .00 7766 400
No. 10. . . . . .00 7766 320
No. 11. . . . . .00 7766 310
No. 12. . . . . .00 7766 300
No. 13. . . . . .00 7766 210
No. 14. . . . . .00 7766 200
No. 15. . . . . .00 7766 100
No. 16. . . . . .00 7766 000

Nazard 2⅔′. 00 0060 000
Nineteenth 1⅓′. 00 0000 060

Octave 4′
No. 1. .00 0804 010
No. 2. .00 0704 010
No. 3. .00 0604 010
Octave Harmonic Diapason 4′.00 0606 045
Octave Major Diapason 4′. . .00 0828 077
Octave Minor Diapason 4′. . .00 0707 066
Octave Phonon 4′. 00 0808 077
Octave Quint 2⅔′. 00 0060 010
Open Diapason 8′
No. 1. .01 8866 540
No. 2. .01 8866 530
No. 3. .01 8866 520
No. 4. .01 8866 510
No. 5. .01 8866 500
No. 6. .01 8866 430
No. 7. .01 8866 420
No. 8. .00 8866 410
No. 9. .01 8866 400
No. 10. . . . . .01 8866 320
No. 11. . . . . .01 8866 310
No. 12. . . . . .01 8866 300
No. 13. . . . . .01 8866 210
No. 14. . . . . .01 8866 200
No. 15. . . . . .01 8866 100
No. 16. . . . . .01 8866 000
No. 17. . . . . .01 8855 430
No. 18. . . . . .00 8855 420
No. 19. . . . . .00 8855 410
No. 20. . . . . .00 8855 400
No. 21. . . . . .00 8855 320
No. 22. . . . . .00 8855 310
No. 23. . . . . .00 8855 300
No. 24. . . . . .00 8855 210
No. 25. . . . . .00 8855 200
No. 26. . . . . .00 8855 100
No. 27. . . . . .00 8855 000
No. 28. . . . . .02 8855 430
No. 29. . . . . .02 8855 420
No. 30. . . . . .02 8855 410
No. 31. . . . . .02 8855 400
No. 32. . . . . .02 8855 320
No. 33. . . . . .02 8855 310
No. 34. . . . . .02 8855 300
No. 35. . . . . .02 8855 210
No. 36. . . . . .02 8855 200
No. 37. . . . . .02 8855 100
No. 38. . . . . .02 8855 000
No. 39. . . . . .00 8844 320
No. 40. . . . . .00 8844 310
No. 41. . . . . .00 8844 300
No. 42. . . . . .00 8844 210
No. 43. . . . . .00 8844 200
No. 44. . . . . .00 8844 100
No. 45. . . . . .00 8844 000

Open Diapason 8′

No. 46	00	8745	423
No. 47	00	8745	422
No. 48	00	8745	421
No. 49	00	8745	420
No. 50	00	8745	411
No. 51	00	8745	410
No. 52	00	8745	400
No. 53	00	8745	323
No. 54	00	8745	322
No. 55	00	8745	312
No. 56	00	8745	212
No. 57	00	8745	121
No. 58	01	7766	540
No. 59	01	7766	530
No. 60	01	7766	520
No. 61	01	7766	510
No. 62	01	7766	500
No. 63	01	7766	430
No. 64	01	7766	420
No. 65	01	7766	410
No. 66	01	7766	400
No. 67	01	7766	320
No. 68	01	7766	310
No. 69	01	7766	300
No. 70	01	7766	210
No. 71	01	7766	200
No. 72	01	7766	100
No. 73	01	7766	000
No. 74	02	7766	540
No. 75	02	7766	530
No. 76	02	7766	520
No. 77	02	7766	510
No. 78	02	7766	500
No. 79	02	7766	430
No. 80	02	7766	420
No. 81	02	7766	410
No. 82	02	7766	400
No. 83	02	7766	320
No. 84	02	7766	310
No, 85	02	7766	300
No. 86	02	7766	210
No. 87	02	7766	200
No. 88	02	7766	100
No. 89	02	7766	000
No. 90	01	7755	430
No. 91	01	7755	420
No. 92	01	7755	410
No. 93	01	7755	400
No. 94	01	7755	320
No. 95	01	7755	310
No. 96	01	7755	300
No. 97	01	7755	210
No. 98	01	7755	200
No. 99	01	7755	100
No. 100	01	7755	000
No. 101	02	7755	430
No. 102	02	7755	420

Open Diapason 8′

No. 103	02	7755	410
No. 104	02	7755	400
No. 105	02	7755	320
No. 106	02	7755	310
No. 107	02	7755	300
No. 108	02	7755	210
No. 109	02	7755	200
No. 110	02	7755	100
No. 111	02	7755	000
No. 112	01	7744	320
No. 113	01	7744	310
No. 114	01	7744	300
No. 115	01	7744	210
No. 116	01	7744	200
No. 117	01	7744	100
No. 118	01	7744	000
No. 119	00	6655	430
No. 120	00	6655	420
No. 121	00	6655	410
No. 122	00	6655	400
No. 123	00	6655	320
No. 124	00	6655	310
No. 125	00	6655	300
No. 126	00	6655	210
No. 127	00	6655	200
No. 128	00	6655	100
No. 129	00	6655	000
No. 130	01	6655	430
No. 131	01	6655	420
No. 132	01	6655	410
No. 133	01	6655	400
No. 134	01	6655	320
No. 135	01	6655	310
No. 136	01	6655	300
No. 137	01	6655	210
No. 138	01	6655	200
No. 139	01	6655	100
No. 140	01	6655	000
No. 141	00	6644	320
No. 142	00	6644	310
No. 143	00	6644	300
No. 144	00	6644	210
No. 145	00	6644	200
No. 146	00	6644	100
No. 147	00	6644	000

Solo Diapason 8′	
No. 1	01 8855 441
No. 2	01 8855 440
No. 3	01 8855 331
No. 4	01 8855 330
No. 5	01 8855 221
No. 6	01 8855 220
No. 7	01 8855 110
Solo Diapason 4′	00 0818 055
Stentor Diapason 8′	
No. 1	01 8877 650
No. 2	01 8877 640
No. 3	01 8877 630
No. 4	01 8877 620
No. 5	01 8877 610
No. 6	01 8877 600
No. 7	01 8877 540
No. 8	01 8877 530
No. 9	01 8877 520
No. 10	01 8877 510
No. 11	01 8877 500
No. 12	01 8877 430
No. 13	01 8877 420
No. 14	01 8877 410
No. 15	01 8877 400
No. 16	01 8877 320
No. 17	01 8877 310
No. 18	01 8877 300
No. 19	01 8877 210
No. 20	01 8877 200
No. 21	01 8877 100
No. 22	01 8877 000

Open Quint 5⅓′	07 0030 010
Prestant 8′	00 7766 332
Prestant 4′	00 0707 064
Prinzipal 8′	
No. 1	00 8876 540
No. 2	00 8876 530
No. 3	00 8876 520
No. 4	00 8876 510
No. 5	00 8876 500
No. 6	00 8876 430
No. 7	00 8876 420
No. 8	00 8876 410
No. 9	00 8876 400
No. 10	00 8876 320
No. 11	00 8876 310
No. 12	00 8876 300
No. 13	00 8876 210
No. 14	00 8876 200
No. 15	00 8876 100
No. 16	00 8876 000
Quint 5⅓′	07 0000 000
Quint Diapason 5⅓′	07 0020 000
Schutz Diapason 8′	
No. 1	00 7755 221
No. 2	00 7755 220
Septadecima 1⅗′	00 0000 600
Seventeenth 1⅗′	00 0000 600
Solo Diapason 16′	
No. 1	85 8544 000
No. 2	85 8533 000
Stopped Diapason 8′ (flute)	
No. 1	00 7010 000
No. 2	00 6010 000

```
Subprinzipal 16′...........71 7110 000
Super Octave 2′
  No. 1....................00 0007 001
  No. 2....................00 0006 001
Super Octave Tierce 1⅗′....00 0000 700
Swell Diapason 8′
  No. 1....................00 7765 430
  No. 2....................00 7765 420
  No. 3....................00 7765 410
  No. 4....................00 7765 400
  No. 5....................00 7765 320
  No. 6....................00 7765 310
  No. 7....................00 7765 300
  No. 8....................00 7765 210
  No. 9....................00 7765 200
  No. 10...................00 7765 100
  No. 11...................00 7765 000


Tertian 1⅓′ and 1⅗′.......00 0000 430
Tierce 1⅗′................00 0000 700
Tierce Diapason 8′.........00 7755 620
Twelfth 2⅔′
  No. 1....................00 0070 000
  No. 2....................00 0060 000
  No. 3....................00 0050 000
Twelfth Major 2⅔′.........00 0080 000
Twelfth Minor 2⅔′.........00 0040 000


Viola Diapason 8′
  No. 1....................00 7786 231
  No. 2....................00 6675 231
  No. 3....................00 5564 121
Violin Diapason 8′
  No. 1....................00 7786 541
  No. 2....................00 6675 431
  No. 3....................00 5564 321


Wood Diapason 16′
  No. 1....................82 7310 000
  No. 2....................82 7311 000
Wood Diapason 8′
  No. 1....................00 7754 320
  No. 2....................00 7754 310
  No. 3....................00 7754 300
  No. 4....................00 7754 210
  No. 5....................00 7754 200
  No. 6....................00 7754 100
  No. 7....................00 7754 000
Wood Diapason 4′
  No. 1....................00 0707 053
  No. 2....................00 0707 054
```

UNASSIGNED BASIC FOUNDATION
NUMBER-ARRANGEMENTS FOR THE ADVANCED STUDENT

The following basic Foundation number-arrangements have not been assigned to any particular name in the Dictionary.   The more advanced student of registration can give them names of his choice.   All are 8' tones:

00 8883 210	00 8755 210	00 8533 210	00 7864 210
00 8882 210	00 8754 210	00 8488 210	00 7863 210
00 8881 210	00 8753 210	00 8487 210	00 7862 210
00 8878 210	00 8752 210	00 8486 210	00 7861 210
00 8868 210	00 8751 210	00 8485 210	00 7858 210
00 8867 210	00 8747 210	00 8484 210	00 7857 210
00 8858 210	00 8688 210	00 8483 210	00 7856 210
00 8857 210	00 8685 210	00 8446 210	00 7787 210
00 8848 210	00 8677 210	00 8445 210	00 7784 210
00 8847 210	00 8676 210	00 8444 210	00 7782 210
00 8846 210	00 8675 210	00 8443 210	00 7781 210
00 8845 210	00 8674 210	00 8442 210	00 7778 210
00 8838 210	00 8668 210	00 8441 210	00 7773 210
00 8837 210	00 8667 210	00 8435 210	00 7772 210
00 8836 210	00 8666 210	00 8434 210	00 7771 210
00 8835 210	00 8665 210	00 8433 210	00 7768 210
00 8834 210	00 8664 210	00 8432 210	00 7767 210
00 8833 210	00 8656 210	00 8431 210	00 7758 210
00 8822 210	00 8655 210	00 8423 210	00 7757 210
00 8788 210	00 8654 210	00 8422 210	00 7756 210
00 8787 210	00 8653 210	00 8412 210	00 7688 210
00 8785 210	00 8644 210	00 8411 210	00 7687 210
00 8784 210	00 8643 210	00 8388 210	00 7686 210
00 8783 210	00 8642 210	00 8387 210	00 7685 210
00 8782 210	00 8641 210	00 8222 210	00 7684 210
00 8781 210	00 8632 210	00 8221 210	00 7683 210
00 8776 210	00 8631 210	00 7886 210	00 7682 210
00 8775 210	00 8622 210	00 7885 210	00 7678 210
00 8774 210	00 8621 210	00 7884 210	00 7676 210
00 8773 210	00 8556 210	00 7883 210	00 7675 210
00 8772 210	00 8555 210	00 7882 210	00 7674 210
00 8768 210	00 8554 210	00 7881 210	00 7673 210
00 8767 210	00 8553 210	00 7878 210	00 7668 210
00 8766 210	00 8552 210	00 7877 210	00 7667 210
00 8765 210	00 8551 210	00 7876 210	00 7666 210
00 8764 210	00 8545 210	00 7875 210	00 7665 210
00 8763 210	00 8544 210	00 7874 210	00 7664 210
00 8762 210	00 8543 210	00 7873 210	00 7663 210
00 8758 210	00 8542 210	00 7867 210	00 7662 210
00 8757 210	00 8535 210	00 7866 210	00 7661 210
00 8756 210	00 8534 210	00 7865 210	00 7658 210

00 7657 210	00 6882 210	00 5552 100	00 3223 100
00 7656 210	00 6878 210	00 5545 100	00 3222 100
00 7655 210	00 6877 210	00 5543 100	00 3221 100
00 7654 210	00 6876 210	00 5542 100	00 3212 100
00 7653 210	00 6875 210	00 5445 100	00 3211 100
00 7652 210	00 6874 210	00 5444 100	00 3123 100
00 7588 210	00 6787 210	00 5443 100	00 3113 100
00 7555 210	00 6786 210	00 5442 100	00 3112 100
00 7554 210	00 6687 210	00 5354 100	00 3111 100
00 7553 210	00 6686 210	00 5344 100	00 2234 100
00 7552 210	00 6685 210	00 5343 100	00 2233 100
00 7545 210	00 6668 210	00 5333 100	00 2232 100
00 7544 210	00 6667 210	00 5332 100	00 2231 000
00 7543 210	00 6665 210	00 5331 100	00 2111 000
00 7542 210	00 6664 210	00 5322 100	00 1122 000
00 7541 210	00 6663 210	00 5321 100	00 1121 000
00 7534 210	00 6662 210	00 4453 100	
00 7533 210	00 6658 210	00 4442 100	
00 7532 210	00 6657 210	00 4441 100	
00 7531 210	00 6656 210	00 4435 100	
00 7488 210	00 6646 210	00 4433 100	
00 7487 210	00 6643 210	00 4432 100	
00 7445 210	00 6642 210	00 4334 100	
00 7444 210	00 6552 210	00 4333 100	
00 7443 210	00 6543 100	00 4332 100	
00 7442 210	00 6542 100	00 4223 100	
00 7433 210	00 6541 100	00 4222 100	
00 7432 210	00 6444 100	00 4221 100	
00 7423 210	00 6443 100	00 4111 100	
00 7422 210	00 6442 100	00 3343 100	
00 7334 210	00 6334 100	00 3342 100	
00 7333 210	00 6333 100	00 3334 100	
00 7332 210	00 6332 100	00 3332 100	
00 7223 210	00 6331 100	00 3331 100	
00 7222 210	00 6222 100	00 3324 100	
00 7112 210	00 6221 100	00 3323 100	
00 7111 210	00 6211 100	00 3322 100	
00 6886 210	00 6111 100	00 3321 100	
00 6885 210	00 5565 100	00 3244 100	
00 6884 210	00 5564 100	00 3243 100	
00 6883 210	00 5554 100	00 3224 100	

THE REED STOPS

Aeolodicon 16'...........44 4421 000

Baritone 8'
No. 1.................00 5555 430
No. 2.................00 5555 420
No. 3.................00 5555 410
No. 4.................00 5555 400
No. 5.................00 5555 320
No. 6.................00 5555 310
No. 7.................00 5555 300
No. 8.................00 5555 210
No. 9.................00 5555 200
No. 10................00 5555 100
No. 11................00 5555 000

Basset-horn 8'
No. 1.................00 4664 320
No. 2.................00 4664 310
No. 3.................00 4664 300
No. 4.................00 4664 210
No. 5.................00 4664 200
No. 6.................00 4664 100
No. 7.................00 4664 000

Bassoon 8'
No. 1.................08 8000 000
No. 2.................07 7000 000
No. 3.................06 6000 000
No. 4.................05 5000 000
No. 5.................04 4000 000
No. 6.................03 3000 000
No. 7.................08 8300 000
No. 8.................08 8200 000
No. 9.................08 8100 000
No. 10................07 7300 000
No. 11................07 7200 000
No. 12................07 7100 000
No. 13................06 6200 000
No. 14................06 6100 000
No. 15................05 5200 000
No. 16................05 5100 000
No. 17................04 4100 000
No. 18................03 3100 000
No. 19................08 8120 000
No. 20................07 7120 000
No. 21................06 6120 000
No. 22................05 5120 000
No. 23................04 4120 000
No. 24................03 3120 000
No. 25................08 8020 000
No. 26................08 8010 000
No. 27................07 7020 000
No. 28................07 7010 000
No. 29................06 6010 000
No. 30................05 5010 000
No. 31................06 8000 000

Bassoon 8'
No. 32................05 7000 000
No. 33................06 8120 000
No. 34................05 7120 000
No. 35................06 8020 000
No. 36................06 8010 000
No. 37................05 7020 000
No. 38................05 7010 000

Bass Tuba (orchestral) 16'
No. 1.................86 7420 000
No. 2.................86 7410 000
Bass Tuba (organ type) 16'
No. 1.................88 8864 000
No. 2.................88 8863 000
†Bass Vox Humana 16'......20 4043 100
Bell Clarinet 8'
No. 1.................00 6173 431
No. 2.................00 6173 430
No. 3.................00 6173 421
No. 4.................00 6173 420
No. 5.................00 6173 410
No. 6.................00 6173 400
No. 7.................00 6173 321
No. 8.................00 6173 320
No. 9.................00 6173 310
No. 10................00 6173 300
No. 11................00 6173 210
No. 12................00 6173 200
No. 13................00 6173 212
No. 14................00 6173 001
Bombarde 16'
No. 1.................86 8400 000
No. 2.................87 8400 000
Bombardon 16'.........88 8410 000
Brass Fanfare 8'
No. 1.................01 5788 870
No. 2.................01 5788 860
No. 3.................01 5788 850
No. 4.................01 5788 840

†Both Tremulant and Chorus Control are needed for the Vox Humana.

Brass Fanfare 8′

No. 5	01 5788 830
No. 6	01 5788 820
No. 7	01 5788 810
No. 8	01 5788 800
No. 9	01 5788 760
No. 10	01 5788 750
No. 11	01 5788 740
No. 12	01 5788 730
No. 13	01 5788 720
No. 14	01 5788 710
No. 15	01 5788 700
No. 16	01 5788 650
No. 17	01 5788 640
No. 18	01 5788 630
No. 19	01 5788 620
No. 20	01 5788 610
No. 21	01 5788 600
No. 22	01 5788 540
No. 23	01 5788 530
No. 24	01 5788 520
No. 25	01 5788 510
No. 26	01 5788 500
No. 27	01 5788 430
No. 28	01 5788 420
No. 29	01 5788 410
No. 30	01 5788 400
No. 31	01 5788 320
No. 32	01 5788 310
No. 33	01 5788 300
No. 34	01 5788 210
No. 35	01 5788 200
No. 36	01 5788 100
No. 37	01 5788 000

Brass Trumpet 8′

No. 1	01 5888 870
No. 2	01 5888 860

Brass Trumpet 8′

No. 3	01 5888 850
No. 4	01 5888 840
No. 5	01 5888 830
No. 6	01 5888 820
No. 7	01 5888 810
No. 8	01 5888 800
No. 9	01 5888 760
No. 10	01 5888 750
No. 11	01 5888 740
No. 12	01 5888 730
No. 13	01 5888 720
No. 14	01 5888 710
No. 15	01 5888 700
No. 16	01 5888 650
No. 17	01 5888 640
No. 18	01 5888 630
No. 19	01 5888 620
No. 20	01 5888 610
No. 21	01 5888 600
No. 22	01 5888 540
No. 23	01 5888 530
No. 24	01 5888 520
No. 25	01 5888 510
No. 26	01 5888 500
No. 27	01 5888 430
No. 28	01 5888 420
No. 29	01 5888 410
No. 30	01 5888 400
No. 31	01 5888 320
No. 32	01 5888 310
No. 33	01 5888 300
No. 34	01 5888 210
No. 35	01 5888 200
No. 36	01 5888 100
No. 37	01 5888 000

Bugle 8′

No. 1	00 5885 430
No. 2	00 5885 420
No. 3	00 5885 410
No. 4	00 5885 400
No. 5	00 5885 320
No. 6	00 5885 310
No. 7	00 5885 300
No. 8	00′ 5885 200
No. 9	00 5885 100
No. 10	00 5885 000

Chalumeau 8′

No. 1	00 5353 321
No. 2	00 5353 320
No. 3	00 5353 310
No. 4	00 5353 300
No. 5	00 5353 200

Chamade (horizontal) **8′**

No. 1	00 5688 760
No. 2	00 5688 750
No. 3	00 5688 740
No. 4	00 5688 730

Chorus Reed 8′

No. 1	00 7777 760
No. 2	00 7777 750
No. 3	00 7777 740
No. 4	00 7777 730
No. 5	00 7777 720
No. 6	00 7777 710
No. 7	00 7777 700
No. 8	00 7777 650
No. 9	00 7777 640
No. 10	00 7777 630
No. 11	00 7777 620
No. 12	00 7777 610
No. 13	00 7777 600
No. 14	00 7777 540
No. 15	00 7777 530
No. 16	00 7777 520
No. 17	00 7777 510
No. 18	00 7777 500
No. 19	00 7777 430
No. 20	00 7777 420
No. 21	00 7777 410
No. 22	00 7777 400
No. 23	00 7777 320
No. 24	00 7777 310
No. 25	00 7777 300
No. 26	00 7777 210
No. 27	00 7777 200
No. 28	00 7777 100
No. 29	00 7777 000

Clarinet 8′

No. 1	00 4160 431
No. 2	00 4160 430
No. 3	00 4160 421
No. 4	00 4160 420
No. 5	00 4160 411
No. 6	00 4160 410
No. 7	00 4160 331
No. 8	00 4160 321
No. 9	00 4160 311
No. 10	00 4160 310
No. 11	00 4160 221
No. 12	00 4160 211
No. 13	00 4160 210
No. 14	00 4160 110
No. 15	00 5160 431
No. 16	00 5160 430
No. 17	00 5160 421
No. 18	00 5160 420
No. 19	00 5160 411
No. 20	00 5160 410
No. 21	00 5160 331
No. 22	00 5160 321
No. 23	00 5160 311
No. 24	00 5160 310
No. 25	00 5160 221
No. 26	00 5160 211
No. 27	00 5160 210
No. 28	00 5160 110
No. 29	00 4161 431
No. 30	00 4161 430
No. 31	00 4161 421
No. 32	00 4161 420
No. 33	00 4161 411
No. 34	00 4161 410
No. 35	00 4161 331
No. 36	00 4161 321
No. 37	00 4161 311
No. 38	00 4161 310
No. 39	00 4161 221
No. 40	00 4161 211
No. 41	00 4161 210
No. 42	00 4161 110
No. 43	00 5161 431
No. 44	00 5161 430
No. 45	00 5161 421

Clarinet 8'
No. 46...................00 5161 420
No. 47...................00 5161 411
No. 48...................00 5161 410
No. 49...................00 5161 331
No. 50...................00 5161 321
No. 51...................00 5161 311
No. 52...................00 5161 310
No. 53...................00 5161 221
No. 54...................00 5161 211
No. 55...................00 5161 210
No. 56...................00 5161 110

Clarion 4'
No. 1....................00 0808 088
No. 2....................00 0707 077
No. 3....................00 0606 066
No. 4....................00 0505 055
No. 5....................00 0506 066
Clarion d'Amour 4'.........00 0304 043
Clarion Sonora 4'..........00 0707 065
Clarion Tuba Harmonic 4'..00 0808 078
Contra Clarinet 16'........54 2220 000
Contra Fagotto 16'.........64 7431 000
Contra French Horn 16'.....72 5200 000
Contra Oboe (organ type) 16'.15 3100 000
Contra Oboe Horn 16'.......37 6500 000
Contra Posaune 16'........78 8721 000
Contra Saxophone 16'......86 7100 000
Contra Trombone 16'.......68 8700 000
Contra Trumpet 16'........67 7721 000
Contra Tuba (orchestral) 16'
No. 1...................86 7420 000
No. 2...................86 7410 000
Contra Tuba (organ type) 16'
No. 1...................88 8864 000
No. 2...................88 8863 000
†Contra Vox Humana 16'....42 7350 000
Cornet 8'
No. 1...................00 5665 540
No. 2...................00 5665 530
No. 3...................00 5665 520
No. 4...................00 5665 510
No. 5...................00 5665 500
No. 6...................00 5665 430
No. 7...................00 5665 420
No. 8...................00 5665 410
No. 9...................00 5665 400
No. 10..................00 5665 320
No. 11..................00 5665 310
No. 12..................00 5665 300
No. 13..................00 5665 210
No. 14..................00 5665 200
No. 15..................00 5665 100
No. 16..................00 5665 000

†Both Tremulant and Chorus Control are needed for the Vox Humana.

Cornet à Pavillon 8′

No. 1	01 4777 760
No. 2	01 4777 750
No. 3	01 4777 740
No. 4	01 4777 730
No. 5	01 4777 720
No. 6	01 4777 710
No. 7	01 4777 700
No. 8	01 4777 650
No. 9	01 4777 640
No. 10	01 4777 630
No. 11	01 4777 620
No. 12	01 4777 610
No. 13	01 4777 600
No. 14	01 4777 540
No. 15	01 4777 530
No. 16	01 4777 520
No. 17	01 4777 510
No. 18	01 4777 500
No. 19	01 4777 430
No. 20	01 4777 420
No. 21	01 4777 410
No. 22	01 4777 400
No. 23	01 4777 320
No. 24	01 4777 310
No. 25	01 4777 300
No. 26	01 4777 210
No. 27	01 4777 200
No. 28	01 4777 100
No. 29	01 4777 000

Cornet d'Amour 8′

No. 1	00 4445 320
No. 2	00 4445 310
No. 3	00 4445 300
No. 4	00 4445 210
No. 5	00 4445 200
No. 6	00 4445 211
No. 7	00 4445 121

Corno d'Amore 8′

No. 1	00 4775 430
No. 2	00 4775 420
No. 3	00 4775 410
No. 4	00 4775 400

Corno d'Amore 8′

No. 5	00 4775 320
No. 6	00 4775 310
No. 7	00 4775 300
No. 8	00 4775 210
No. 9	00 4775 200
No. 10	00 4775 100
No. 11	00 4775 000

Corno di Bassetto 8′

No. 1	00 7141 421
No. 2	00 7141 420
No. 3	00 7141 410
No. 4	00 7141 310
No. 5	00 7141 210

Corno Dolce 8′

No. 1	00 4544 321
No. 2	00 4544 320
No. 3	00 4544 212
No. 4	00 4544 211
No. 5	00 4544 121

Cornopean 8′

No. 1	00 5666 650
No. 2	00 5666 640
No. 3	00 5666 630
No. 4	00 5666 620
No. 5	00 5666 610
No. 6	00 5666 600
No. 7	00 5666 540
No. 8	00 5666 530
No. 9	00 5666 520
No. 10	00 5666 510
No. 11	00 5666 500
No. 12	00 5666 430
No. 13	00 5666 420
No. 14	00 5666 410
No. 15	00 5666 400
No. 16	00 5666 320
No. 17	00 5666 310
No. 18	00 5666 300
No. 19	00 5666 210
No. 20	00 5666 200
No. 21	00 5666 100
No. 22	00 5666 000

English Horn 8'

No. 1	00 3682 342
No. 2	00 3682 341
No. 3	00 3682 332
No. 4	00 3682 331
No. 5	00 3682 323
No. 6	00 3682 232
No. 7	00 3682 242
No. 8	00 3682 241
No. 9	00 3682 321
No. 10	00 3682 210
No. 11	00 3682 211
No. 12	00 2583 342
No. 13	00 2583 341
No. 14	00 2583 332
No. 15	00 2583 331
No. 16	00 2583 323
No. 17	00 2583 232
No. 18	00 2583 242
No. 19	00 2583 241
No. 20	00 2583 321
No. 21	00 2583 210
No. 22	00 2583 211

Cromorne 8'

No. 1	00 6050 321
No. 2	00 6050 320
No. 3	00 6050 310
No. 4	00 6050 300
No. 5	00 6050 210
No. 6	00 6050 200
No. 7	00 6050 100
No. 8	00 6050 000

Cro Orlo en Chamade 8'

No. 1	00 5688 760
No. 2	00 5688 750
No. 3	00 4688 740
No. 4	00 4688 730

Double Clarinet 16'	54 2220 000
Double French Horn 16'	72 5200 000
Double Oboe (organ type) 16'	15 3100 000
Double Oboe Horn 16'	37 6500 000
Double Saxophone 16'	86 7100 000
Double Trumpet 16'	67 7721 000

Double Tuba (orchestral) 16'

No. 1	86 7420 000
No. 2	86 7410 000

Double Tuba (organ type) 16'

No. 1	88 8864 000
No. 2	88 8863 000
Double Tuba Harmonic 16'	88 8875 000
†Double Vox Humana 16'	32 6250 000
Dulcian 16'	44 2210 000
Dulcian 8'	00 4242 010

Echo Oboe 8'

No. 1	00 2360 100
No. 2	00 2360 210
No. 3	00 2360 110
Echo Waldhorn 8'	00 4241 110
Egyptian Bazu 8'	00 5482 210

Egyptian Horn 8'

No. 1	00 5686 431
No. 2	00 5686 430
No. 3	00 5686 421
No. 4	00 5686 420

English Tuba 8'	00 6878 630
Euphone 16'	44 4320 000
Euphone 8'	00 5553 010

Euphonium 16'

No. 1	75 8500 000
No. 2	75 8400 000
No. 3	75 8300 000
No. 4	75 8200 000
Fagotto 8'	00 6744 100

†Both Tremulant and Chorus Control are needed for the Vox Humana.

Fanfare 8′

No. 1	01 4888 870
No. 2	01 4888 860
No. 3	01 4888 850
No. 4	01 4888 840
No. 5	01 4888 830
No. 6	01 4888 820
No. 7	01 4888 810
No. 8	01 4888 800
No. 9	01 4888 760
No. 10	01 4888 750
No. 11	01 4888 740
No. 12	01 4888 730
No. 13	01 4888 720
No. 14	01 4888 710
No. 15	01 4888 700
No. 16	01 4888 650
No. 17	01 4888 640
No. 18	01 4888 630
No. 19	01 4888 620
No. 20	01 4888 610
No. 21	01 4888 600
No. 22	01 4888 540
No. 23	01 4888 530
No. 24	01 4888 520
No. 25	01 4888 510
No. 26	01 4888 500
No. 27	01 4888 430
No. 28	01 4888 420
No. 29	01 4888 410
No. 30	01 4888 400
No. 31	01 4888 320
No. 32	01 4888 310
No. 33	01 4888 300
No. 34	01 4888 210
No. 35	01 4888 200
No. 36	01 4888 100
No. 37	01 4888 000

Field Trumpet 8′

No. 1	01 4788 870
No. 2	01 4788 860
No. 3	01 4788 850
No. 4	01 4788 840

Field Trumpet 8′

No. 5	01 4788 830
No. 6	01 4788 820
No. 7	01 4788 810
No. 8	01 4788 800
No. 9	01 4788 760
No. 10	01 4788 750
No. 11	01 4788 740
No. 12	01 4788 730
No. 13	01 4788 720
No. 14	01 4788 710
No. 15	01 4788 700
No. 16	01 4788 650
No. 17	01 4788 640
No. 18	01 4788 630
No. 19	01 4788 620
No. 20	01 4788 610
No. 21	01 4788 600
No. 22	01 4788 540
No. 23	01 4788 530
No. 24	01 4788 520
No. 25	01 4788 510
No. 26	01 4788 500
No. 27	01 4788 430
No. 28	01 4788 420
No. 29	01 4788 410
No. 30	01 4788 400
No. 31	01 4788 320
No. 32	01 4788 310
No. 33	01 4788 300
No. 34	01 4788 210
No. 35	01 4788 200
No. 36	01 4788 100
No. 37	01 4788 000

Flügel Horn 8′

No. 1	00 5777 650
No. 2	00 5777 640
No. 3	00 5777 630
No. 4	00 5777 620
No. 5	00 5777 610
No. 6	00 5777 600
No. 7	00 5777 540
No. 8	00 5777 530
No. 9	00 5777 520
No. 10	00 5777 510
No. 11	00 5777 500
No. 12	00 5777 430
No. 13	00 5777 420
No. 14	00 5777 410
No. 15	00 5777 400
No. 16	00 5777 320
No. 17	00 5777 310
No. 18	00 5777 300
No. 19	00 5777 210
No. 20	00 5777 200
No. 21	00 5777 100
No. 22	00 5777 000

French Bugle 8′

No. 1	01 6887 760
No. 2	01 6887 750
No. 3	01 6887 740
No. 4	01 6887 730
No. 5	01 6887 720
No. 6	01 6887 710
No. 7	01 6887 700
No. 8	01 6887 650
No. 9	01 6887 640
No. 10	01 6887 630
No. 11	01 6887 620
No. 12	01 6887 610
No. 13	01 6887 600
No. 14	01 6887 540
No. 15	01 6887 530
No. 16	01 6887 520
No. 17	01 6887 510
No. 18	01 6887 500
No. 19	01 6887 430
No. 20	01 6887 420
No. 21	01 6887 410
No. 22	01 6887 400
No. 23	01 6887 320
No. 24	01 6887 310
No. 25	01 6887 300
No. 26	01 6887 210
No. 27	01 6887 200
No. 28	01 6887 100

French Horn 8′

No. 1	00 6554 322
No. 2	00 6554 321
No. 3	00 6554 320
No. 4	00 6554 211
No. 5	00 6554 210
No. 6	00 6554 200
No. 7	00 6554 121
No. 8	00 6554 110
No. 9	00 6553 100
No. 10	00 6553 010
No. 11	00 6553 322
No. 12	00 6553 321
No. 13	00 6553 320
No. 14	00 6553 211
No. 15	00 6553 210
No. 16	00 6553 200
No. 17	00 6555 121
No. 18	00 6555 110
No. 19	00 6555 010
No. 20	00 6555 100
No. 21	00 6555 322
No. 22	00 6555 321
No. 23	00 6555 320
No. 24	00 6555 211
No. 25	00 6544 210
No. 26	00 6544 200
No. 27	00 6544 121
No. 28	00 6544 110
No. 29	00 6544 010
No. 30	00 6544 100
No. 31	00 6544 322
No. 32	00 6544 321
No. 33	00 6545 320
No. 34	00 6545 211
No. 35	00 6545 210
No. 36	00 6545 200
No. 37	00 6545 121
No. 38	00 6545 110
No. 39	00 6545 010
No. 40	00 6545 100
No. 41	00 6645 320
No. 42	00 6645 311
No. 43	00 6645 312
No. 44	00 6645 342
No. 45	00 6645 221
No. 46	00 6645 220
No. 47	00 6645 313
No. 48	00 6645 213
No. 49	00 6563 221
No. 50	00 6563 211

French Trumpet 8'

No. 1	00 7888 882
No. 2	00 7888 881
No. 3	00 7888 880
No. 4	00 7888 872
No. 5	00 7888 871
No. 6	00 7888 870
No. 7	00 7888 862
No. 8	00 7888 861
No. 9	00 7888 860
No. 10	00 7888 851
No. 11	00 7888 850
No. 12	00 7888 840
No. 13	00 7888 830
No. 14	00 7888 820
No. 15	00 7888 810
No. 16	00 7888 800
No. 17	00 7888 761
No. 18	00 7888 760
No. 19	00 7888 751
No. 20	00 7888 750
No. 21	00 7888 740
No. 22	00 7888 730
No. 23	00 7888 720
No. 24	00 7888 710
No. 25	00 7888 700
No. 26	00 7888 651
No. 27	00 7888 650
No. 28	00 7888 640
No. 29	00 7888 630
No. 30	00 7888 620
No. 31	00 7888 610
No. 32	00 7888 600
No. 33	00 7888 540
No. 34	00 7888 530
No. 35	00 7888 520
No. 36	00 7888 510
No. 37	00 7888 500
No. 38	00 7888 430
No. 39	00 7888 420

French Trumpet 8'

No. 40	00 7888 410
No. 41	00 7888 400
No. 42	00 7888 320
No. 43	00 7888 310
No. 44	00 7888 300
No. 45	00 7888 210
No. 46	00 7888 200
No. 47	00 7888 100
No. 48	00 7888 000

Grand Ophicleide 8' 04 8888 882

Gross Trumpet 8'

No. 1	00 5888 870
No. 2	00 5888 860
No. 3	00 5888 850

Gross Trumpet 8′

No. 4	00 5888 840
No. 5	00 5888 830
No. 6	00 5888 820
No. 7	00 5888 810
No. 8	00 5888 800
No. 9	00 5888 760
No. 10	00 5888 750
No. 11	00 5888 740
No. 12	00 5888 730
No. 13	00 5888 720
No. 14	00 5888 710
No. 15	00 5888 700
No. 16	00 5888 650
No. 17	00 5888 640
No. 18	00 5888 630
No. 19	00 5888 620
No. 20	00 5888 610
No. 21	00 5888 600
No. 22	00 5888 540
No. 23	00 5888 530
No. 24	00 5888 520
No. 25	00 5888 510
No. 26	00 5888 500
No. 27	00 5888 430
No. 28	00 5888 420
No. 29	00 5888 410
No. 30	00 5888 400
No. 31	00 5888 320
No. 32	00 5888 310
No. 33	00 5888 300
No. 34	00 5888 210
No. 35	00 5888 200
No. 36	00 5888 100
No. 37	00 5888 000

Harmonic Oboe 8′

No. 1	00 2383 312
No. 2	00 2383 212

Harmonic Trumpet 8′

No. 1	03 7888 870
No. 2	03 7888 860
No. 3	03 7888 850
No. 4	03 7888 840
No. 5	03 7888 830
No. 6	03 7888 820
No. 7	03 7888 810
No. 8	03 7888 800
No. 9	03 7888 760
No. 10	03 7888 750
No. 11	03 7888 740
No. 12	03 7888 730
No. 13	03 7888 720
No. 14	03 7888 710
No. 15	03 7888 700
No. 16	03 7888 650
No. 17	00 7888 640
No. 18	03 7888 630
No. 19	03 7888 620
No. 20	03 7888 610
No. 21	03 7888 600
No. 22	03 7888 540
No. 23	03 7888 530
No. 24	03 7888 520
No. 25	03 7888 510
No. 26	03 7888 500
No. 27	03 7888 430
No. 28	03 7888 420
No. 29	03 7888 410
No. 30	03 7888 400
No. 31	03 7888 320
No. 32	03 7888 310
No. 33	03 7888 300
No. 34	03 7888 210
No. 35	03 7888 200
No. 36	03 7888 100
No. 37	03 7888 000

Harmonic Tuba 8′

No. 1	03 8888 870
No. 2	03 8888 860
No. 3	03 8888 850
No. 4	03 8888 840
No. 5	03 8888 830
No. 6	03 8888 820
No. 7	03 8888 810
No. 8	03 8888 800
No. 9	03 8888 760
No. 10	03 8888 750
No. 11	03 8888 740
No. 12	03 8888 730
No. 13	03 8888 720
No. 14	03 8888 710
No. 15	03 8888 700
No. 16	03 8888 650
No. 17	03 8888 640
No. 18	03 8888 630
No. 19	03 8888 620
No. 20	03 8888 610
No. 21	03 8888 600
No. 22	03 8888 540
No. 23	03 8888 530
No. 24	03 8888 520
No. 25	03 8888 510
No. 26	03 8888 500
No. 27	03 8888 430
No. 28	03 8888 420
No. 29	03 8888 410
No. 30	03 8888 400
No. 31	03 8888 320
No. 32	03 8888 310
No. 33	03 8888 300
No. 34	03 8888 210
No. 35	03 8888 200
No. 36	03 8888 100
No. 37	03 8888 000

Heckelphone 8′

No. 1	00 4554 430
No. 2	00 4554 420
No. 3	00 4554 410
No. 4	00 4554 400
No. 5	00 4554 320
No. 6	00 4554 310
No. 7	00 4554 300
No. 8	00 4554 210
No. 9	00 4554 200
No. 10	00 4554 100
No. 11	00 4554 000

Hunting Horn 8′

No. 1	00 7456 320
No. 2	00 7465 310
No. 3	00 7465 300
No. 4	00 7465 210
No. 5	00 7465 200
No. 6	00 7465 100
No. 7	00 7465 000

*Kinura 8′

No. 1	00 0152 786
No. 2	00 0162 786
No. 3	00 0172 786
No. 4	00 0183 786

Labial Tuba 8′

No. 1	00 8786 430
No. 2	00 8786 420
No. 3	00 8786 410
No. 4	00 8786 400
No. 5	00 8786 320

Labial Tuba 8'
No. 6................00 8786 310
No. 7................00 8786 300
No. 8................00 8786 210
No. 9................00 8786 200
No. 10...............00 8786 100

Mellophone 8'
No. 1................00 5776 540
No. 2................00 5776 530
No. 3................00 5776 520
No. 4................00 5776 510
No. 5................00 5776 500
No. 6................00 5776 430
No. 7................00 5776 420
No. 8................00 5776 410
No. 9................00 5776 400
No. 10...............00 5776 320
No. 11...............00 5776 310
No. 12...............00 5776 300
No. 13...............00 5776 210

Military Fanfare 8'
No. 1................01 7788 760
No. 2................01 7788 750
No. 3................01 7788 740
No. 4................01 7788 730
No. 5................01 7788 720
No. 6................01 7788 710
No. 7................01 7788 700
No. 8................01 7788 650
No. 9................01 7788 640
No. 10...............01 7788 630
No. 11...............01 7788 620
No. 12...............01 7788 610
No. 13...............01 7788 600
No. 14...............01 7788 540
No. 15...............01 7788 530
No. 16...............01 7788 520
No. 17...............01 7788 510
No. 18...............01 7788 500
No. 19...............01 7788 430
No. 20...............01 7788 420
No. 21...............01 7788 410
No. 22...............01 7788 400
No. 23...............01 7788 320
No. 24...............01 7788 310
No. 25...............01 7788 300
No. 26...............01 7788 210
No. 27...............01 7788 200
No. 28...............01 7788 100
No. 29...............01 7788 000

Musette 8'
No. 1................00 2270 213
No. 2................00 2270 313
No. 3................00 2270 312
Musette Mirabilis 8'
No. 1................00 2370 310
No. 2................00 2370 210
Oboe (organ type) 8'
No. 1................00 4571 110
No. 2................00 4571 010
No. 3................00 4571 011
No. 4................00 4571 120
No. 5................00 4571 210
No. 6................00 4571 321
No. 7................00 4571 320
Oboe d'Amore 8'
No. 1................00 2350 310
No. 2................00 2350 300
No. 3................00 2350 210
No. 4................00 2350 120
Oboe Horn 8'
No. 1................00 4675 310
No. 2................00 4675 300
No. 3................00 4675 210
No. 4................00 4675 200
No. 5................00 4675 100
No. 6................00 4675 000
No. 7................00 4675 010
No. 8................00 3675 310
No. 9................00 3675 210
No. 10...............00 3675 110
Oboe Major 8'...........00 3482 321
Octave Oboe 4'
No. 1................00 0203 071
No. 2................00 0203 061
Ophicleide 8'
No. 1................04 8888 881
No. 2................04 8888 880
No. 3................04 8888 870
No. 4................04 8888 860
No. 5................04 8888 850
No. 6................04 8888 840
No. 7................04 8888 830
No. 8................04 8888 820
Orchestral Oboe 8'
No. 1................00 2472 243
No. 2................00 2472 342
No. 3................00 2472 341

Orchestral Oboe 8'

No. 4	00 2472 241
No. 5	00 2472 143
No. 6	00 2472 142
No. 7	00 2472 144
No. 8	00 2472 021
No. 9	00 2472 012
No. 10	00 2472 112
No. 11	00 2472 132
No. 12	00 2472 051
No. 13	00 2472 321
No. 14	00 2472 431
No. 15	00 1271 243
No. 16	00 1271 342
No. 17	00 1271 341
No. 18	00 1271 241
No. 19	00 1271 143
No. 20	00 1271 142
No. 21	00 1271 144
No. 22	00 1271 021
No. 23	00 1271 012
No. 24	00 1271 112
No. 25	00 1271 132
No. 26	00 1271 051
No. 27	00 1271 321
No. 28	00 1271 431
No. 29	00 3472 243
No. 30	00 3472 342
No. 31	00 3472 341
No. 32	00 3472 241
No. 33	00 3472 143
No. 34	00 3472 142
No. 35	00 3472 144
No. 36	00 3472 021
No. 37	00 3472 012
No. 38	00 3472 112
No. 39	00 3472 132
No. 40	00 3472 051
No. 41	00 3472 321
No. 42	00 3472 431
No. 43	00 3572 243
No. 44	00 3572 342
No. 45	00 3572 341
No. 46	00 3572 241
No. 47	00 3572 143
No. 48	00 3572 142
No. 49	00 3572 144
No. 50	00 3572 021
No. 51	00 3572 012
No. 52	00 3572 112
No. 53	00 3572 132
No. 54	00 3572 051
No. 55	00 3572 321
No. 56	00 3572 431
No. 57	00 3581 431
No. 58	00 3581 241
No. 59	00 3581 251
No. 60	00 3581 252

Orchestral Trumpet 8'

No. 1	00 6788 880
No. 2	00 6788 870
No. 3	00 6788 860
No. 4	00 6788 850
No. 5	00 6788 840
No. 6	00 6788 830
No. 7	00 6788 820
No. 8	00 6788 810
No. 9	00 6788 800
No. 10	00 6788 760
No. 11	00 6788 750
No. 12	00 6788 740
No. 13	00 6788 730
No. 14	00 6788 720
No. 15	00 6788 710
No. 16	00 6788 700
No. 17	00 6788 650
No. 18	00 6788 640
No. 19	00 6788 630
No. 20	00 6788 620
No. 21	00 6788 610

Orchestral Trumpet 8'

No. 22	00 6788 600
No. 23	00 6788 540
No. 24	00 6788 530
No. 25	00 6788 520
No. 26	00 6788 510
No. 27	00 6788 500
No. 28	00 6788 430
No. 29	00 6788 420
No. 30	00 6788 410
No. 31	00 6788 400
No. 32	00 6788 320
No. 33	00 6788 310
No. 34	00 6788 300
No. 35	00 6788 210
No. 36	00 6788 200
No. 37	00 6788 100
No. 38	00 6788 000

Oriental Reed 8'

No. 1	00 1371 654
No. 2	00 1371 543
No. 3	00 1371 432

Oriental Reed 8'

No. 4	00 1371 321
No. 5	00 1371 324
No. 6	00 1582 654
No. 7	00 1582 543
No. 8	00 1582 432
No. 9	00 1582 321
No. 10	00 1582 324

Physharmonica 8'

No. 1	01 4443 210
No. 2	01 4443 200
No. 3	01 4443 100
No. 4	01 4443 000

Posaune 8'

No. 1	00 7887 430
No. 2	00 7887 420
No. 3	00 7887 410
No. 4	00 7887 400
No. 5	00 7887 320
No. 6	00 7887 310
No. 7	00 7887 300
No. 8	00 7887 210
No. 9	00 7887 200
No. 10	00 7887 100
No. 11	00 7887 000

Post Horn 8'

No. 1	00 6677 650
No. 2	00 6677 640
No. 3	00 6677 630
No. 4	00 6677 620
No. 5	00 6677 610
No. 6	00 6677 600
No. 7	00 6677 540
No. 8	00 6677 530
No. 9	00 6677 520
No. 10	00 6677 510
No. 11	00 6677 500
No. 12	00 6677 430
No. 13	00 6677 420
No. 14	00 6677 410
No. 15	00 6677 400
No. 16	00 6677 320
No. 17	00 6677 310
No. 18	00 6677 300
No. 19	00 6677 210
No. 20	00 6677 200
No. 21	00 6677 100
No. 22	00 6677 000

Reed Chorus

No. 1	83 8888 886
No. 2	83 8888 885
No. 3	83 8888 883
No. 4	83 8888 883
No. 5	83 8888 882
No. 6	83 8888 881
No. 7	83 8888 880
No. 8	83 8888 876
No. 9	83 8888 875
No. 10	83 8888 874
No. 11	83 8888 873
No. 12	83 8888 872
No. 13	83 8888 871
No. 14	83 8888 870
No. 15	63 8888 886
No. 16	63 8888 885
No. 17	63 8888 884
No. 18	63 8888 883
No. 19	63 8888 882
No. 20	63 8888 881
No. 21	63 8888 880
No. 22	63 8888 876
No. 23	63 8888 875
No. 24	63 8888 874
No. 25	63 8888 873
No. 26	63 8888 872
No. 27	63 8888 871
No. 28	63 8888 870
No. 29	63 8888 865
No. 30	63 8888 864
No. 31	63 8888 863
No. 32	63 8888 862
No. 33	63 8888 861
No. 34	63 8888 860

Sarrusophone 16′

No. 1	45 4210 000
No. 2	45 4200 000
No. 3	45 4100 000
No. 4	45 4000 000
No. 5	45 4010 000
No. 6	45 4020 000

Saxophone 8'			
No. 1	01	8762	431
No. 2	01	8762	430
No. 3	01	8762	420
No. 4	01	8762	410
No. 5	01	8762	400
No. 6	01	8762	321
No. 7	01	8762	320
No. 8	01	8762	310
No. 9	01	8762	300
No. 10	01	8762	210
No. 11	01	8762	200
No. 12	01	8762	100
No. 13	01	8762	010
No. 14	01	8761	431
No. 15	01	8761	430
No. 16	01	8761	420
No. 17	01	8761	410
No. 18	01	8761	400
No. 19	01	8761	321
No. 20	01	8761	320
No. 21	01	8761	310
No. 22	01	8761	300
No. 23	01	8761	210
No. 24	01	8761	200
No. 25	01	8761	100
No. 26	01	8761	010
No. 27	01	8761	120
No. 28	02	8762	120
No. 29	02	8761	120

Solo Tuba 16'	85	8630	000
Solo Tuba 8'			
No. 1	01	7777	770
No. 2	01	7777	760
No. 3	01	7777	750
No. 4	01	7777	740
No. 5	01	7777	730
No. 6	01	7777	720
No. 7	01	7777	710
No. 8	01	7777	700
No. 9	01	7777	650
No. 10	01	7777	640
No 11	01	7777	630
No. 12	01	7777	620
No. 13	01	7777	610
No. 14	01	7777	600
No. 15	01	7777	540
No. 16	01	7777	530
No. 17	01	7777	520
No. 18	01	7777	510
No. 19	01	7777	500
No. 20	01	7777	430
No. 21	01	7777	420
No. 22	01	7777	410
No. 23	01	7777	400
No. 24	01	7777	320
No. 25	01	7777	310
No. 26	01	7777	300
No. 27	01	7777	210
No. 28	01	7777	200
No. 29	01	7777	100
No. 30	01	7777	000

Solo Tuba 4'	00	0708	077

†Solo Vox Humana 8′

No. 1	00 4630 100
No. 2	00 4630 200
No. 3	00 4630 210
No. 4	00 4630 321
No. 5	00 4630 010
No. 6	00 4630 012

Tromba 16′

No. 1	85 8631 000
No. 2	85 8621 000
No. 3	85 8620 000

Tromba Clarion 4′ 00 0808 056

Trombone 8′

No. 1	01 8777 760
No. 2	01 8777 750
No. 3	01 8777 740
No. 4	01 8777 730
No. 5	01 8777 720
No. 6	01 8777 710
No. 7	01 8777 700
No. 8	01 8777 650
No. 9	01 8777 640
No. 10	01 8777 630
No. 11	01 8777 620
No. 12	01 8777 610
No. 13	01 8777 600
No. 14	01 8777 540
No. 15	01 8777 530
No. 16	01 8777 520
No. 17	01 8777 510
No. 18	01 8777 500
No. 19	01 8777 430
No. 20	01 8777 420
No. 21	01 8777 410
No. 22	01 8777 400
No. 23	01 8777 320
No. 24	01 8777 310
No. 25	01 8777 300
No. 26	01 8777 210
No. 27	01 8777 200
No. 28	01 8777 100
No. 29	01 8777 000

Trompette en Chamade 8′

No. 1	00 5688 760
No. 2	00 5688 750
No. 3	00 5688 740
No. 4	00 5688 730

Trumpet (organ type) 8′

No. 1	00 7677 540
No. 2	00 7677 530
No. 3	00 7677 520
No. 4	00 7677 510
No. 5	00 7677 500
No. 6	00 7677 430
No. 7	00 7677 420
No. 8	00 7677 410
No. 9	00 7677 400
No. 10	00 7677 320
No. 11	00 7677 310
No. 12	00 7677 300
No. 13	00 7677 210
No. 14	00 6777 200
No. 15	00 7677 100
No. 16	00 7677 000

Trumpet Fanfare 8′

No. 1	01 6788 880
No. 2	01 6788 870
No. 3	01 6788 860
No. 4	01 6788 850
No. 5	01 6788 840
No. 6	01 6788 830
No. 7	01 6788 820
No. 8	01 6788 810
No. 9	01 6788 800
No. 10	01 6788 760
No. 11	01 6788 750
No. 12	01 6788 740
No. 13	01 6788 730
No. 14	01 6788 720
No. 15	01 6788 710
No. 16	01 6788 700
No. 17	01 6788 650
No. 18	01 6788 640
No. 19	01 6788 630
No. 20	01 6788 620
No. 21	01 6788 610
No. 22	01 6788 600
No. 23	01 6788 540
No. 24	01 6788 530
No. 25	01 6788 520
No. 26	01 6788 510
No. 27	01 6788 500
No. 28	01 6788 430
No. 29	01 6788 420
No. 30	01 6788 410
No. 31	01 6788 400
No. 32	01 6788 320
No. 33	01 6788 310
No. 34	01 6788 300

†Both Tremulant and Chorus Control are needed for the Vox Humana.

Trumpet Fanfare 8′
No. 35..................01 6788 210
No. 36..................01 6788 200
No. 37..................01 6788 100
No. 38..................01 6788 000

Trumpet Imperial 8′
No. 24..................00 6688 530
No. 25..................00 6688 520
No. 26..................00 6688 510
No. 27..................00 6688 500
No. 28..................00 6688 430
No. 29..................00 6688 420
No. 30..................00 6688 410
No. 31..................00 6688 400
No. 32..................00 6688 320
No. 33..................00 6688 310
No. 34..................00 6688 300
No. 35..................00 6688 210
No. 36..................00 6688 200
No. 37..................00 6688 100
No. 38..................00 6688 000

Tuba (organ type) 16′
No. 1..................88 8864 000
No. 2..................88 8863 000

Tuba (organ type) 8′
No. 1..................03 6888 880
No. 2..................03 6888 870
No. 3..................03 6888 860
No. 4..................03 6888 850
No. 5..................03 6888 840
No. 6..................03 6888 830
No. 7..................03 6888 820
No. 8..................03 6888 810
No. 9..................03 6888 800
No. 10..................03 6888 760
No. 11..................03 6888 750
No. 12..................03 6888 740
No. 13..................03 6888 730
No. 14..................03 6888 720
No. 15..................03 6888 710
No. 16..................03 6888 700
No. 17..................03 6888 650
No. 18..................03 6888 640
No. 19..................03 6888 630
No. 20..................03 6888 620
No. 21..................03 6888 610
No. 22..................03 6888 600
No. 23..................03 6888 540
No. 24..................03 6888 530

Trumpet Imperial 8′
No. 1..................00 6688 880
No. 2..................00 6688 870
No. 3..................00 6688 860
No. 4..................00 6688 850
No. 5..................00 6688 840
No. 6..................00 6688 830
No. 7..................00 6688 820
No. 8..................00 6688 810
No. 9..................00 6688 800
No. 10..................00 6688 760
No. 11..................00 6688 750
No. 12..................00 6688 740
No. 13..................00 6688 730
No. 14..................00 6688 720
No. 15..................00 6688 710
No. 16..................00 6688 700
No. 17..................00 6688 650
No. 18..................00 6688 640
No. 19..................00 6688 630
No. 20..................00 6688 620
No. 21..................00 6688 610
No. 22..................00 6688 600
No. 23..................00 6688 540

Tuba (organ type) 8′

No. 25	03 6888 520
No. 26	03 6888 510
No. 27	03 6888 500
No. 28	03 6888 430
No. 29	03 6888 420
No. 30	03 6888 410
No. 31	03 6888 400
No. 32	03 6888 320
No. 33	03 6888 310
No. 34	03 6888 300
No. 35	03 6888 210
No. 36	03 6888 200
No. 37	03 6888 100
No. 38	03 6888 000
No. 39	02 6888 880
No. 40	02 6888 870
No. 41	02 6888 860
No. 42	02 6888 850
No. 43	02 6888 840
No. 44	02 6888 830
No. 45	02 6888 820
No. 46	02 6888 810
No. 47	02 6888 800
No. 48	02 6888 760
No. 49	02 6888 750
No. 50	02 6888 740
No. 51	02 6888 730
No. 52	02 6888 720
No. 53	02 6888 710
No. 54	02 6888 700
No. 55	02 6888 650
No. 56	02 6888 640
No. 57	02 6888 630
No. 58	02 6888 620
No. 59	02 6888 610
No. 60	02 6888 600
No. 61	02 6888 540
No. 62	02 6888 530
No. 63	02 6888 520
No. 64	02 6888 510
No. 65	02 6888 500
No. 66	02 6888 430
No. 67	02 6888 420
No. 68	02 6888 410
No. 69	02 6888 400
No. 70	02 6888 320
No. 71	02 6888 310
No. 72	02 6888 300
No. 73	02 6888 210
No. 74	02 6888 200
No. 75	02 6888 100
No. 76	02 6888 000
No. 77	01 6888 880
No. 78	01 6888 870
No. 79	01 6888 860
No. 80	01 6888 850
No. 81	01 6888 840

Tuba (organ type) 8′

No. 82	01 6888 830
No. 83	01 6888 820
No. 84	01 6888 810
No. 85	01 6888 800
No. 86	01 6888 760
No. 87	01 6888 750
No. 88	01 6888 740
No. 89	01 6888 730
No. 90	01 6888 720
No. 91	01 6888 710
No. 92	01 6888 700
No. 93	01 6888 650
No. 94	01 6888 640
No. 95	01 6888 630
No. 96	01 6888 620
No. 97	01 6888 610
No. 98	01 6888 600
No. 99	01 6888 540
No. 100	01 6888 530
No. 101	01 6888 520
No. 102	01 6888 510
No. 103	01 6888 500
No. 104	01 6888 430
No. 105	01 6888 420
No. 106	01 6888 410
No. 107	01 6888 400
No. 108	01 6888 320
No. 109	01 6888 310
No. 110	01 6888 300
No. 111	01 6888 210
No. 112	01 6888 200
No. 113	01 6888 100
No. 114	01 6888 000
No. 115	00 6888 880
No. 116	00 6888 870
No. 117	00 6888 860
No. 118	00 6888 850
No. 119	00 6888 840
No. 120	00 6888 830
No. 121	00 6888 820
No. 122	00 6888 810
No. 123	00 6888 800
No. 124	00 6888 760
No. 125	00 6888 750
No. 126	00 6888 740
No. 127	00 6888 730
No. 128	00 6888 720
No. 129	00 6888 710
No. 130	00 6888 700
No. 131	00 6888 650
No. 132	00 6888 640
No. 133	00 6888 630
No. 134	00 6888 620
No. 135	00 6888 610
No. 136	00 6888 600
No. 137	00 6888 540
No. 138	00 6888 530

Tuba (organ type) 8′

No. 139	00	6888	520
No. 140	00	6888	510
No. 141	00	6888	500
No. 142	00	6888	430
No. 143	00	6888	420
No. 144	00	6888	410
No. 145	00	6888	400
No. 146	00	6888	320
No. 147	00	6888	310
No. 148	00	6888	300
No. 149	00	6888	210
No. 150	00	6888	200
No. 151	00	6888	100
No. 152	00	6888	000
No. 153	02	5888	880
No. 154	02	5888	870
No. 155	02	5888	860
No. 156	02	5888	850
No. 157	02	5888	840
No. 158	02	5888	830
No. 159	02	5888	820
No. 160	02	5888	810
No. 161	02	5888	800
No. 162	02	5888	760
No. 163	02	5888	750
No. 164	02	5888	740
No. 165	02	5888	730
No. 166	02	5888	720
No. 167	02	5888	710
No. 168	02	5888	700
No. 169	02	5888	650
No. 170	02	5888	640
No. 171	02	5888	630
No. 172	02	5888	620
No. 173	02	5888	610
No. 174	02	5888	600
No. 175	02	5888	540
No. 176	02	5888	530
No. 177	02	5888	520
No. 178	02	5888	510
No. 179	02	5888	500
No. 180	02	5888	430
No. 181	02	5888	420
No. 182	02	5888	410
No. 183	02	5888	400
No. 184	02	5888	320
No. 185	02	5888	310
No. 186	02	5888	300
No. 187	02	5888	210
No. 188	02	5888	200
No. 189	02	5888	100
No. 190	02	5888	000
No. 191	00	4555	430
No. 192	00	4555	420
No. 193	00	4555	410
No. 194	00	4555	400
No. 195	00	4555	320

Tuba (organ type) 8′

No. 196	00	4555	310
No. 197	00	4555	300
No. 198	00	4555	210
No. 199	00	4555	200
No. 200	00	4555	100
No. 201	00	4555	000

Tuba Chorus

No. 1	84	8888	886
No. 2	84	8888	885
No. 3	84	8888	884
No. 4	84	8888	883
No. 5	84	8888	882
No. 6	84	8888	881

Tuba Imperial 8′

No. 24	01 7888 530
No. 25	01 7888 520
No. 26	01 7888 510
No. 27	01 7888 500
No. 28	01 7888 430
No. 29	01 7888 420
No. 30	01 7888 410
No. 31	01 7888 400
No. 32	01 7888 320
No. 33	01 7888 310
No. 34	01 7888 300
No. 35	01 7888 210
No. 36	01 7888 200
No. 37	01 7888 100
No. 38	01 7888 000

Tuba d'Amore 8′

No. 1	00 4563 443
No. 2	00 4563 332
No. 3	00 4563 221
No. 4	00 4563 342
No. 5	00 4563 243
No. 6	00 4563 241
No. 7	00 4563 142
No. 8	00 4563 111
No. 9	00 4563 112
No. 10	00 4563 121
No. 11	00 4563 132
No. 12	00 4563 123

Tuba Imperial 8′

No. 1	01 7888 880
No. 2	01 7888 870
No. 3	01 7888 860
No. 4	01 7888 850
No. 5	01 7888 840
No. 6	01 7888 830
No. 7	01 7888 820
No. 8	01 7888 810
No. 9	01 7888 800
No. 10	01 7888 760
No. 11	01 7888 750
No. 12	01 7888 740
No. 13	01 7888 730
No. 14	01 7888 720
No. 15	01 7888 710
No. 16	01 7888 700
No. 17	01 7888 650
No. 18	01 7888 640
No. 19	01 7888 630
No. 20	01 7888 620
No. 21	01 7888 610
No. 22	01 7888 600
No. 23	01 7888 540

Tuba Magna 8′

No. 1	01 8888 880
No. 2	01 8888 870
No. 3	01 8888 860
No. 4	01 8888 850
No. 5	01 8888 840
No. 6	01 8888 830
No. 7	01 8888 820
No. 8	01 8888 810
No. 9	01 8888 800
No. 10	01 8888 760
No. 11	01 8888 750
No. 12	01 8888 740
No. 13	01 8888 730
No. 14	01 8888 720
No. 15	01 8888 710
No. 16	01 8888 700
No. 17	01 8888 650
No. 18	01 8888 640
No. 19	01 8888 630
No. 20	01 8888 620

Tuba Magna 8′

No. 21	01 8888	610
No. 22	01 8888	600
No. 23	01 8888	540
No. 24	01 8888	530
No. 25	01 8888	520
No. 26	01 8888	510
No. 27	01 8888	500
No. 28	01 8888	430
No. 29	01 8888	420
No. 30	01 8888	410
No. 31	01 8888	400
No. 32	01 8888	320
No. 33	01 8888	310
No. 34	01 8888	300
No. 35	01 8888	210
No. 36	01 8888	200
No. 37	01 8888	100
No. 38	01 8888	000

Tuba Major 8′

No. 17	02 8888	650
No. 18	02 8888	640
No. 19	02 8888	630
No. 20	02 8888	620
No. 21	02 8888	610
No. 22	02 8888	600
No. 23	02 8888	540
No. 24	02 8888	530
No. 25	02 8888	520
No. 26	02 8888	510
No. 27	02 8888	500
No. 28	02 8888	430
No. 29	02 8888	420
No. 30	02 8888	410
No. 31	02 8888	400
No. 32	02 8888	320
No. 33	02 8888	310
No. 34	02 8888	300
No. 35	02 8888	210
No. 36	02 8888	200
No. 37	02 8888	100
No. 38	02 8888	000

Tuba Major 8′

No. 1	02 8888	880
No. 2	02 8888	870
No. 3	02 8888	860
No. 4	02 8888	850
No. 5	02 8888	840
No. 6	02 8888	830
No. 7	02 8888	820
No. 8	02 8888	810
No. 9	02 8888	800
No. 10	02 8888	760
No. 11	02 8888	750
No. 12	02 8888	740
No. 13	02 8888	730
No. 14	02 8888	720
No. 15	02 8888	710
No. 16	02 8888	700

Tuba Minor 8′

No. 1	00 4444	430
No. 2	00 4444	420
No. 3	00 4444	410
No. 4	00 4444	400
No. 5	00 4444	320
No. 6	00 4444	310
No. 7	00 4444	300
No. 8	00 4444	210
No. 9	00 4444	200
No. 10	00 4444	100
No. 11	00 4444	000

Tuba Mirabilis 8′

No. 1	00 8888 870
No. 2	00 8888 860
No. 3	00 8888 850
No. 4	00 8888 840
No. 5	00 8888 830
No. 6	00 8888 820
No. 7	00 8888 810
No. 8	00 8888 800
No. 9	00 8888 760
No. 10	00 8888 750
No. 11	00 8888 740
No. 12	00 8888 730
No. 13	00 8888 720
No. 14	00 8888 710
No. 15	00 8888 700
No. 16	00 8888 650
No. 17	00 8888 640
No. 18	00 8888 630
No. 19	00 8888 620
No. 20	00 8888 610
No. 21	00 8888 600
No. 22	00 8888 540
No. 23	00 8888 530
No. 24	00 8888 520
No. 25	00 8888 510
No. 26	00 8888 500
No. 27	00 8888 430
No. 28	00 8888 420
No. 29	00 8888 410
No. 30	00 8888 400
No. 31	00 8888 320
No. 32	00 8888 310
No. 33	00 8888 300
No. 34	00 8888 210
No. 35	00 8888 200
No. 36	00 8888 100
No. 37	00 8888 000

Tuba Sonora 8′

No. 1	02 7788 880
No. 2	02 7788 870
No. 3	02 7788 860
No. 4	02 7788 850
No. 5	02 7788 840
No. 6	02 7788 830
No. 7	02 7788 820
No. 8	02 7788 810
No. 9	02 7788 800
No. 10	02 7788 760
No. 11	02 7788 750
No. 12	02 7788 740
No. 13	02 7788 730
No. 14	02 7788 720
No. 15	02 7788 710
No. 16	02 7788 700
No 17	02 7788 650
No. 18	02 7788 640
No. 19	02 7788 630
No. 20	02 7788 620
No. 21	02 7788 610
No. 22	02 7788 600
No. 23	02 7788 540
No. 24	02 7788 530
No. 25	02 7788 520
No. 26	02 7788 510
No. 27	02 7788 500
No. 28	02 7788 430
No. 29	02 7788 420
No. 30	02 7788 410
No. 31	02 7788 400
No. 32	02 7788 320
No. 33	02 7788 310
No. 34	02 7788 300
No. 35	02 7788 210
No. 36	02 7788 200
No. 37	02 7788 100
No. 38	02 7788 000

Vox Humana 8'

No. 23	00 2520	123
No. 24	00 2520	124
No. 25	00 2520	135
No. 26	00 2520	134
No. 27	00 2520	136
No. 28	00 2520	145
No. 29	00 2520	143
No. 30	00 2520	285
No. 31	00 3630	012
No. 32	00 3630	112
No. 33	00 3630	123
No. 34	00 3630	124
No. 35	00 3630	135
No. 36	00 3630	134
No. 37	00 3630	136
No. 38	00 3630	145
No. 39	00 3630	143
No. 40	00 3630	285
No. 41	00 4730	124
No. 42	00 4730	125
No. 43	00 4730	135
No. 44	00 4730	136
No. 45	00 4730	137
No. 46	00 4730	147
No. 47	00 4730	148
No. 48	00 4730	245
No. 49	00 4730	346
No. 50	00 4730	457
No. 51	00 2450	123
No. 52	00 2470	234
No. 53	00 2560	345
No. 54	00 2650	456
No. 55	00 2680	567
No. 56	00 2770	678
No. 57	00 2040	356
No. 58	00 2050	357
No. 59	00 2060	236
No. 60	00 2070	148

†Vox Humana 16' 33 6045 000

†Vox Humana 8'

No. 1	00 4720	012
No. 2	00 4720	112
No. 3	00 4720	123
No. 4	00 4720	124
No. 5	00 4720	135
No. 6	00 4720	134
No. 7	00 4720	136
No. 8	00 4720	145
No. 9	00 4720	143
No. 10	00 4720	285
No. 11	00 3620	012
No. 12	00 3620	112
No. 13	00 3620	123
No. 14	00 3620	124
No. 15	00 3620	135
No. 16	00 3620	134
No. 17	00 3620	136
No. 18	00 3620	145
No. 19	00 3620	143
No. 20	00 3620	285
No. 21	00 2520	012
No. 22	00 2520	112

Waldhorn 8'

No. 1	00 4343	210
No. 2	00 4343	200
No. 3	00 4343	100
No. 4	00 4343	110
No. 5	00 4343	211

†Both Tremulant and Chorus Control are needed for the Vox Humana.

UNASSIGNED BASIC REED
NUMBER-ARRANGEMENTS FOR THE ADVANCED STUDENT

The following basic Tuba and Trumpet number-arrangements have not been assigned to any particular name in the Dictionary.   You may add names of organ-stop Tubas to them.   Those with lighter tone are Trumpets.

```
04 7888 654
03 7777 432
03 6788 432
03 6777 543
02 6777 654
01 6777 765
00 6777 876
02 6688 543
01 6688 753
01 6677 653
01 6666 431
00 6666 321
01 5777 543
01 5688 742
01 5677 432
00 5677 432
00 5566 432
02 4888 753
00 4888 632
00 4788 752
00 4777 742
02 4688 752
01 4688 753
00 4688 432
00 4677 632
00 4666 432
00 4588 642
00 4577 642
00 4455 321
01 3888 764
00 3888 642
01 3788 632
00 3788 432
00 3344 321
00 3333 321
```

THE FLUTE STOPS

Accompanimental Flute 8′

No. 1	00 8870 000
No. 2	00 8860 000
No. 3	00 8850 000
No. 4	00 8780 000
No. 5	00 8770 000
No. 6	00 8680 000
No. 7	00 8670 000
No. 8	00 8660 000
No. 9	00 8580 000
No. 10	00 8570 000
No. 11	00 8560 000
No. 12	00 8550 000
No. 13	00 8460 000
No. 14	00 8450 000
No. 15	00 8440 000
No. 16	00 7760 000
No. 17	00 7570 000
No. 18	00 7470 000
No. 19	00 7450 000
No. 20	00 7440 000
No. 21	00 7130 000
No. 22	00 6650 000
No. 23	00 6640 000
No. 24	00 6560 000
No. 25	00 6550 000
No. 26	00 6460 000
No. 27	00 6450 000
No. 28	00 6340 000
No. 29	00 5450 000
No. 30	00 5250 000
No. 31	00 4350 000
No. 32	00 4330 000
No. 33	00 3220 000
No. 34	00 2230 000
No. 35	00 8800 000
No. 36	00 8700 000
No. 37	00 8600 000
No. 38	00 8500 000
No. 39	00 8400 000
No. 40	00 8300 000
No. 41	00 8200 000
No. 42	00 8100 000

Amorosa 8′	00 5120 000
Amorosa 4′	00 0501 020
Bass Flute 16′	51 4000 000
Bauerflöte 8′	00 3010 000
Bauerflöte 4′	00 0300 010
Blockflöte 8′	00 5310 000
Blockflöte 4′	00 0503 010
Bordunalflöte 8′	00 6230 100
Bourdon 16′	
No. 1	81 0000 000
No. 2	71 0000 000
No. 3	61 0000 000
Bourdonecho 16′	41 0000 000
Célestina 4′	00 0304 010
Chimney Flute 8′	
No. 1	00 5230 100
No. 2	00 5220 100
Clarabella 8′	
No. 1	00 6210 000
No. 2	00 5210 000
Claribel Flute 4′	
No. 1	00 0602 010
No. 2	00 0502 010
Clear Flute 4′	00 0602 000
Concert Flute 4′	00 0400 020
Concert Piccolo 2′	00 0004 000
Cone Flute 8′	00 4320 000
Contra Flute 16′	31 0000 000
Cordedain 4′	00 0600 030
Cor de Nuit 8′	00 3120 000
Corno Flute 8′	00 5430 000
Divinare 4′	00 0400 010
Dolcan 8′	00 7210 000
Doppelflöte 8′	00 6310 000
Doppelrohrflöte 8′	00 5320 000
Doppelrohrgedeckt 8′	00 6410 000
Doppelspitzflöte 8′	00 5121 000
Double Melodia 16′	62 5000 000
Duophone 8′	00 4410 000
Echo Bourdon 16′	30 0000 000
Echoflöte 8′	00 2100 000
Echoflöte 4′	00 0201 000

Feldflöte 4'..................	00 0603 000
Fernflöte 8'.................	00 1000 000
Fernflöte 4'.................	00 0100 000
Fife 2'......................	00 0005 001
Fife 1'......................	00 0000 005
Fifteenth 2'................	00 0003 000
Flachflöte 8'...............	00 3420 000
Flachflöte 4'...............	00 0304 020
Flageolet 2'................	00 0007 001
Flageolet 1'................	00 0000 007
Flageolet Harmonique 2'....	00 0005 004
Flautino 2'.................	00 0005 002
Flautone 8'.................	00 7520 000
Flute (organ type) 16'......	50 3000 000
Flute (organ type) 8'.......	00 5300 000
Flute (organ type) 4'.......	00 0503 000
Flute (organ type) 2'.......	00 0005 003
Flûte d'Amour 8'............	00 4120 000
Flûte d'Amour 4'............	00 0401 020
Forest Flute 8'.............	00 6120 000
Forest Flute 4'.............	00 0601 020

Full Flute 8'

No. 1...................	00 8750 000
No. 2...................	00 8740 000
No. 3...................	00 8730 000
No. 4...................	00 8720 000
No. 5...................	00 8710 000

Gedecktflöte 4'.............	00 0702 000

Grossflöte 8'

No. 1...................	00 7640 000
No. 2...................	00 7630 000
No. 3...................	00 7620 000
No. 4...................	00 7610 000
Grossgedeckt 16'..........	80 1000 000

Harmonic Flute 8'..........	00 4521 000
Harmonic Flute 4'..........	00 0405 021
Harmonic Piccolo 2'........	00 0004 003
Hellflöte 8'................	00 6400 000
Hohlflöte 8'................	00 7320 000
Hohlflöte 4'................	00 0703 020
Hohlflötenbass 16'..........	72 3000 000
Hohlschelle 8'..............	00 4230 000
Humangedeckt 8'...........	00 6300 000

Jubalflöte 8'...............	00 6320 000
Jubalflöte 4'...............	00 0603 020

Keraulophone 8'

No. 1...................	00 6432 000
No. 2...................	00 5432 000
Kleingedeckt 8'............	00 4200 000
Kleingedeckt 4'............	00 0400 000

Lieblichbordun 16'.........	70 0000 000
Lieblichflöte 4'............	00 0400 000

Lieblichgedeckt 8'

No. 1...................	00 8000 000
No. 2...................	00 7000 000

Magic Flute 8'.............	00 3520 000

Major Flute 8'

No. 1...................	00 6430 000
No. 2...................	00 6420 000
Melodia 16'...............	62 5000 000

Melodia 8'

No. 1...................	00 6520 000
No. 2...................	00 6510 000
Minor Flute 8'.............	00 2000 000
Minor Flute 4'.............	00 0200 000

Nachthorn 8'...............	00 3120 000
Nazard 2⅔'................	00 0030 000
Nineteenth 1⅓'............	00 0000 030

Oboe Flute 8'..............	00 3241 000
Octave Flute 4'............	00 0300 000

Open Flute 8'

No. 1...................	00 7510 000
No. 2...................	00 7410 000

*Orchestral Flute 8'

No. 1...................	00 3831 000
No. 2...................	00 3821 000
No. 3...................	00 3811 000
No. 4...................	00 2811 000
No. 5...................	00 1731 000
No. 6...................	00 1721 000
No. 7...................	00 1711 000

Orchestral Piccolo 2'

No. 1...................	00 0006 004
No. 2...................	00 0006 003

Pastorita 8'...............	00 3120 000

Philomela 8'

No. 1...................	00 7430 000
No. 2...................	00 7420 000

Piccolo 2'

No. 1...................	00 0006 004
No. 2...................	00 0006 003
Piccolo d'Amour 2'........	00 0004 001
Portunalflöte 8'...........	00 3230 000

Prinzipalflöte 8'

No. 1...................	00 8540 000
No. 2...................	00 7540 000

Prinzipalflöte 4'

No. 1...................	00 0805 040
No. 2...................	00 0705 040
Pyramidflöte 8'............	00 5630 000
Pyramidflöte 4'............	00 0506 030

*Querflöte 8'..............	00 3811 000
Quint 5⅓'.................	03 0000 000
Quintadena 8'.............	00 5330 000
Quintaten 8'..............	00 5340 000

*Chorus Control indispensable.

Quint Flute 5⅓'	03	0000 000
Quint Flute 2⅔'	03	0030 000
Rauschflöte 1⅓' and 2'	00	0003 030
Rauschpfeife 1⅓, 2', and 2⅔'	00	0033 030
Rauschquinte 2' and 2⅔'	00	0033 000
Ripienflöte 8'	00	4310 000
Rohrflöte 8'	00	5230 100
Sanftflöte 8'	00	3200 000
Schöngedeckt 8'	00	5000 000
Seraphonflöte 8'	00	8520 000
Seventeenth 1⅗'	00	0000 300
Sifflöte 2'	00	0004 004
Sifflöte 1'	00	0000 004
Soave 8'	00	6200 000
Spillflöte 8'	00	4210 000
Spillflöte 4'	00	0402 010
Spillflöte 2'	00	0004 002
Spire Flute 8'	00	5230 100
Spitzflöte 8'	00	3441 100
Stentorflöte 8'	00	7530 000
Stentorphone 8'		
No. 1	00	8640 000
No. 2	00	6540 000
Stopped Diapason 8'		
No. 1	00	7010 000
No. 2	00	6010 000
Stopped Flute 8'		
No. 1	00	5030 000
No. 2	00	5020 000
No. 3	00	5010 000
Stopped Flute 4'	00	0500 010
Suabe Flute 4'	00	0502 020
Sub Bass 16'	83	0000 000
Super Octave 2'	00	0003 000
Super Octave Flute 2'	00	0003 000
Tibia 16'	73	0000 000
Tibia 8'	00	7030 000
Tibia 4'	00	0700 030
Tibia Angusta 8'	00	7400 000
Tibia Bifara 8'	00	5220 000
Tibia Clausa 8'		
No. 1	00	8030 000
No. 2	00	8020 000
Tibia Dura 8'		
No. 1	00	8420 000
No. 2	00	8410 000
Tibia Flute 4'	00	0700 030
Tibia Major 8'	00	8010 000
Tibia Minor 8'	00	4010 000
Tibia Mollis 8'	00	3210 000
Tibia Octave 4'	00	0700 030
Tibia Plena 8'		
No. 1	00	8320 000
No. 2	00	8310 000

Tibia Profunda 16'	73	0000 000
Tibia Rex 8'	00	8040 000
Tibia Rurestris 8'	00	3010 000
Tibia Sylvestris 8'	00	5230 000
Tibia Vulgaris 8'	00	5310 000
Tierce 1⅗'	00	0000 300
Traversflöte 8'	00	3521 000
Traversflöte 4'	00	0305 021
Twelfth 2⅔'	00	0030 000
Twenty-second 1'	00	0000 003
Unda Maris 8'	00	2430 000
Voce Flebile 16'	72	0000 000
Vogelflöte 4'	00	0406 000
Voix Séraphique 8'	00	8430 000
Waldflöte 8'		
No. 1	00	5240 000
No. 2	00	4130 000
Wienerflöte 8'	00	3421 000
Willow Flute 8'	00	5420 000
Wooden Open Flute 8'		
No. 1	00	8840 000
No. 2	00	8830 000
No. 3	00	8820 000
No. 4	00	8810 000
No. 5	00	8530 000
No. 6	00	8510 000
No. 7	00	8220 000
No. 8	00	8210 000
No. 9	00	8120 000
No. 10	00	8110 000
No. 11	00	7750 000
No. 12	00	7740 000
No. 13	00	7730 000
No. 14	00	7720 000
No. 15	00	7710 000
No. 16	00	7340 000
No. 17	00	7330 000
No. 18	00	7310 000
No. 19	00	7120 000
No. 20	00	7110 000
No. 21	00	6630 000
No. 22	00	6620 000
No. 23	00	6610 000
No. 24	00	6530 000
No. 25	00	6440 000
No. 26	00	6330 000
No. 27	00	6230 000
No. 28	00	6220 000
No. 29	00	5530 000
No. 30	00	5520 000
No. 31	00	5510 000
No. 32	00	5110 000
No. 33	00	4220 000
No. 34	00	4110 000

Wooden Open Flute 8′
No. 35..................00 3110 000
No. 36..................00 2110 000

Zartflöte 8′
No. 1...................00 6431 000
No. 2...................00 5431 000

Wooden Stopped Flute 8′
No. 1...................00 8070 000
No. 2...................00 8060 000
No. 3...................00 8050 000
No. 4...................00 7060 000
No. 5...................00 7050 000
No. 6...................00 7040 000
No. 7...................00 6040 000
No. 8...................00 6030 000
No. 9...................00 6020 000
No. 10..................00 5040 000
No. 11..................00 4030 000
No. 12..................00 4020 000
No. 13..................00 3020 000
No. 14..................00 2010 000
No. 15..................00 1010 000

UNASSIGNED BASIC FLUTE
NUMBER-ARRANGEMENTS FOR THE ADVANCED STUDENT

The following basic Flute number arrangements have not been assigned to any particular name in the Dictionary. The more advanced student of registration can give them names of his choice and add them to his notebook. No endings should be added to the last three positions, as Flute tone is simple in structure. All of the following are 8' Flute tones:

00 8760 000	00 6450 000	00 3350 000	00 1240 000	00 2800 000
00 8650 000	00 6180 000	00 3340 000	00 1230 000	00 2700 000
00 8630 000	00 6170 000	00 3320 000	00 1220 000	00 2600 000
00 8620 000	00 6110 000	00 3310 000	00 1210 000	00 2500 000
00 8610 000	00 6080 000	00 3080 000	00 1040 000	00 2400 000
00 8480 000	00 6070 000	00 3070 000	00 1030 000	00 2300 000
00 8470 000	00 6060 000	00 3060 000	00 1020 000	00 2200 000
00 8380 000	00 5570 000	00 3050 000	00 7800 000	00 1800 000
00 8370 000	00 5560 000	00 3040 000	00 7700 000	00 1700 000
00 8360 000	00 5540 000	00 3030 000	00 7600 000	00 1600 000
00 8350 000	00 5460 000	00 2540 000	00 7500 000	00 1500 000
00 8340 000	00 5440 000	00 2530 000	00 7400 000	00 1400 000
00 8330 000	00 5410 000	00 2510 000	00 7300 000	00 1300 000
00 8280 000	00 5080 000	00 2450 000	00 7200 000	00 1200 000
00 8270 000	00 5070 000	00 2440 000	00 7100 000	00 1100 000
00 8260 000	00 5060 000	00 2420 000	00 6800 000	00 6000 000
00 8250 000	00 5050 000	00 2410 000	00 6700 000	00 4000 000
00 8240 000	00 4550 000	00 2340 000	00 6600 000	00 3000 000
00 8230 000	00 4540 000	00 2330 000	00 6500 000	
00 8180 000	00 4530 000	00 2320 000	00 6100 000	
00 8080 000	00 4520 000	00 2310 000	00 5800 000	
00 7880 000	00 4510 000	00 2210 000	00 5700 000	
00 7870 000	00 4430 000	00 2140 000	00 5600 000	
00 7860 000	00 4360 000	00 2130 000	00 5500 000	
00 7850 000	00 4340 000	00 2120 000	00 5400 000	
00 7840 000	00 4260 000	00 2080 000	00 5200 000	
00 7830 000	00 4220 000	00 2070 000	00 5100 000	
00 7820 000	00 4150 000	00 2060 000	00 4800 000	
00 7810 000	00 4140 000	00 2050 000	00 4700 000	
00 7780 000	00 4080 000	00 2040 000	00 4600 000	
00 7660 000	00 4070 000	00 2030 000	00 4500 000	
00 7650 000	00 4060 000	00 2020 000	00 4400 000	
00 7370 000	00 4050 000	00 1410 000	00 4300 000	
00 7360 000	00 4040 000	00 1340 000	00 4100 000	
00 7350 000	00 3450 000	00 1330 000	00 3500 000	
00 7220 000	00 3440 000	00 1320 000	00 3400 000	
00 6550 000	00 3430 000	00 1310 000	00 3300 000	
00 6540 000	00 3410 000	00 1250 000	00 3100 000	

THE STRING STOPS

Aeoline 8′
No. 1	00 1221 111
No. 2	00 1221 110
No. 3	00 1221 100
No. 4	00 1221 101
No. 5	00 1221 010
No. 6	00 1221 011
No. 7	00 1221 001
No. 8	00 1221 000
*Aeoline Céleste 8′	00 1121 110
*Aeoline Vibrato 8′	00 1231 110

Bass Violin 16′
No. 1	15 4421 000
No 2	15 4420 000
No. 3	15 4311 000
No. 4	15 4310 000
No. 5	15 4300 000

Bell Gamba 8′
No. 1	00 3486 543
No. 2	00 3486 542
No. 3	00 3486 541
No. 4	00 3486 433
No. 5	00 3486 432
No. 6	00 3486 431
No. 7	00 3486 422
No. 8	00 3486 433
No. 9	00 3486 442
No. 10	00 3486 434
No. 11	00 3488 343
No. 12	00 3486 423
No. 13	00 3486 342
No. 14	00 3486 311
No. 15	00 3486 312
No. 16	00 3486 213
No. 17	00 3486 122
No. 18	00 3486 121
No. 19	00 3486 212
No. 20	00 3486 214
No. 21	00 3486 313
No. 22	00 3486 314
No. 23	00 3486 310
No. 24	00 3486 410
No. 25	00 3486 210
No. 26	00 3486 122
No. 27	00 3486 123

*Céleste 8′ ... 00 2564 311

'Cello 8′
No. 1	00 3564 423
No. 2	00 3564 422
No. 3	00 3564 421
No. 4	00 3564 434

'Cello 8′
No. 5	00 3564 443
No. 6	00 3564 435
No. 7	00 3564 534
No. 8	00 3564 401
No. 9	00 3564 402
No. 10	00 3564 415
No. 11	00 3564 414
No. 12	00 3564 413
No. 13	00 3564 412
No. 14	00 3564 411
No. 15	00 3564 333
No. 16	00 3564 324
No. 17	00 3564 322
No. 18	00 3564 311
No. 19	00 3564 323
No. 20	00 3564 325
No. 21	00 3564 445
No. 22	00 3564 321
No. 23	00 3564 320
No. 24	00 3564 211
No. 25	00 3564 213
No. 26	00 3564 212
No. 27	00 3564 121

*Chorus Control indispensable.

'Cello Pomposa 8'
No. 1 . . . . 00 5684 434
No. 2 . . . . 00 5684 443
No. 3 . . . . 00 5684 442
No. 4 . . . . 00 5684 444
No. 5 . . . . 00 5684 425
No. 6 . . . . 00 5684 426
No. 7 . . . . 00 5684 354
No. 8 . . . . 00 5684 554
No. 9 . . . . 00 5684 355
No. 10 . . . . 00 5684 454
No. 11 . . . . 00 5684 353
No. 12 . . . . 00 5684 542
No. 13 . . . . 00 5684 541
No. 14 . . . . 00 5684 342

'Cello Phonon 8'
No. 1 . . . . 00 4584 545
No. 2 . . . . 00 4584 543
No. 3 . . . . 00 4584 544
No. 4 . . . . 00 4584 542
No. 5 . . . . 00 4584 546
No. 6 . . . . 00 4584 454
No. 7 . . . . 00 4584 453
No. 8 . . . . 00 4584 452
No. 9 . . . . 00 4584 434
No. 10 . . . . 00 4584 433
No. 11 . . . . 00 4584 435
No. 12 . . . . 00 4584 423
No. 13 . . . . 00 4584 431
No. 14 . . . . 00 4584 344
No. 15 . . . . 00 4584 343
No. 16 . . . . 00 4584 342
No. 17 . . . . 00 4584 420
No. 18 . . . . 00 4584 243
No. 19 . . . . 00 4584 244
No. 20 . . . . 00 4584 234

'Cello Sordo 8' 00 1555 200
*'Cello Sordo Céleste 8' 00 1555 222
Cone Gamba 8'
No. 1 . . . . 00 2575 431
No. 2 . . . . 00 2575 430
No. 3 . . . . 00 2575 421
No. 4 . . . . 00 2575 420
No. 5 . . . . 00 2575 410
Contra Dulciana 16'
No, 1 . . . . 66 6000 000
No. 2 . . . . 55 5000 000

Contra Gamba 16'
No. 1 . . . . 48 5434 210
No. 2 . . . . 48 5432 111
Contra Gemshorn 16'
No. 1 . . . . 32 4110 000
No. 2 . . . . 32 4100 000

Dulcet 4' 00 0505 050
Dulciana 8'
No. 1 . . . . 00 8880 000
No. 2 . . . . 00 7770 000
No. 3 . . . . 00 6660 000
No. 4 . . . . 00 5550 000
No. 5 . . . . 00 4440 000
No. 6 . . . . 00 3330 000
No. 7 . . . . 00 2220 000

*Chorus Control indispensable.

Echo 'Cello 8'
  No. 1....................00 1222 110
  No. 2....................00 1222 010
*Echo 'Cello Céleste 8'......00 1222 111
Echo Dulcet 4'............00 0101 010
Echo Dulciana 8'..........00 1110 000
Echo Gamba 8'............00 2332 100
Echo Gemshorn 8'..........00 1421 000
Echo Violin 8'
  No. 1....................00 1243 321
  No. 2....................00 1243 320
  No. 3....................00 1243 310
  No. 4....................00 1243 300
  No. 5....................00 1243 210
  No. 6....................00 1243 200
  No. 7....................00 1243 100
  No. 8....................00 1243 010
  No. 9....................00 1243 001

Erzähler 8'
  No. 1....................00 4543 210
  No. 2....................00 4543 200
  No. 3....................00 4543 100
Ethereal Violin 8'
  No. 1....................00 1242 321
  No. 2....................00 1242 320
  No. 3....................00 1242 310
  No. 4....................00 1242 300
  No. 5....................00 1242 210
  No. 6....................00 1242 200
  No. 7....................00 1242 100
  No. 8....................00 1242 010
  No. 9....................00 1242 001
  No. 10...................00 1242 121
*Ethereal Violin Céleste 8'..00 1242 331

Gamba 8'
  No. 1....................00 3473 453
  No. 2....................00 3474 452
  No. 3....................00 3474 451
  No. 4....................00 3474 353
  No. 5....................00 3474 352
  No. 6....................00 3474 351
  No. 7....................00 3474 254

Gamba 8'
  No. 8....................00 3474 253
  No. 9....................00 3474 252
  No. 10...................00 3474 251
  No. 11...................00 3474 153
  No. 12...................00 3474 354
  No. 13...................00 3474 355
  No. 14...................00 3474 353
  No. 15...................00 3474 352
  No. 16...................00 3474 344
  No. 17...................00 3474 342
  No. 18...................00 3474 341
  No. 19...................00 3474 234
  No. 20...................00 3474 232
  No. 21...................00 3474 233
  No. 22...................00 3474 231
  No. 23...................00 3474 243
  No. 24...................00 3474 242
  No. 25...................00 3474 241
  No. 26...................00 3474 121
  No. 27...................00 3474 131
  No. 28...................00 3474 141

Gamba Celesta 8'
  No. 1....................00 3474 342
  No. 2....................00 3474 231

Gambenbass 16'............37 4432 100
Gambette 4'...............00 0304 074

*Chorus Control indispensable.

Gemshorn 8′
No. 1	00 4741 321
No. 2	00 4741 320
No. 3	00 4741 310
No. 4	00 4741 300
No. 5	00 4741 210
No. 6	00 4741 200
No. 7	00 4741 100
No. 8	00 4741 000
No. 9	00 4741 001

Grand Violin 8′
No. 1	00 4685 454
No. 2	00 4685 453
No. 3	00 4685 345
No. 4	00 4685 344
No. 5	00 4685 342
No. 6	00 4685 341
No. 7	00 4685 354
No. 8	00 4685 353
No. 9	00 4685 352
No. 10	00 4685 351
No. 11	00 4685 434
No. 12	00 4685 436
No. 13	00 4685 435
No. 14	00 4685 543
No. 15	00 4685 432
No. 16	00 4685 321
No. 17	00 4685 323
No. 18	00 4685 322
No. 19	00 4685 312
No. 20	00 4685 311
No. 21	00 4685 313

*Gemshorn Céleste 8′.......00 4741 111

German Gamba 8′
No. 1	00 3483 323
No. 2	00 3483 332
No. 3	00 3483 331
No. 4	00 3483 322
No. 5	00 3483 324
No. 6	00 3483 234
No. 7	00 3483 232
No. 8	00 3483 143
No. 9	00 3483 132
No. 10	00 3483 142
No. 11	00 3483 033
No. 12	00 3483 032
No. 13	00 3483 022
No. 14	00 3483 021
No. 15	00 3483 011

Gross 'Cello 8′
No. 1	00 4757 543
No. 2	00 4757 542
No. 3	00 4757 541
No. 4	00 4757 435
No. 5	00 4757 433
No. 6	00 4757 432
No. 7	00 4757 431
No. 8	00 4757 422
No. 9	00 4757 412
No. 10	00 4757 342
No. 11	00 4757 333
No. 12	00 4757 332
No. 13	00 4757 331
No. 14	00 3464 543
No. 15	00 3464 542
No. 16	00 3464 451
No. 17	00 3464 453
No. 18	00 3464 452
No. 19	00 3464 434
No. 20	00 3464 444

*Chorus Control indispensable.

Gross 'Cello 8'

No. 21	00 3464 443
No. 22	00 3464 442
No. 23	00 3464 441
No. 24	00 3464 342
No. 25	00 3464 341
No. 26	00 3464 340
No. 27	00 3464 424
No. 28	00 3464 423
No. 29	00 3463 321
No. 30	00 3463 310

Gross Gamba 8'

No. 21	00 4786 310
No. 22	00 4786 300
No. 23	00 4786 210
No. 24	00 4786 200
No. 25	00 4786 100
No. 26	00 4786 020
No. 27	00 4786 010
No. 28	00 4786 121

Gross Gamba 8'

No 1	00 4786 543
No. 2	00 4786 542
No. 3	00 4786 541
No. 4	00 4786 540
No. 5	00 4786 532
No. 6	00 4786 531
No. 7	00 4786 530
No. 8	00 4786 521
No. 9	00 4786 520
No. 10	00 4786 510
No. 11	00 4786 500
No. 12	00 4786 432
No. 13	00 4786 431
No. 14	00 4786 430
No. 15	00 4786 421
No. 16	00 4786 420
No. 17	00 4786 410
No. 18	00 4786 400
No. 19	00 4786 321
No. 20	00 4786 320

Gross Gemshorn 8'

No. 1	00 6866 543
No. 2	00 6866 542
No. 3	00 6866 541
No. 4	00 6866 540
No. 5	00 6866 532
No. 6	00 6866 531
No. 7	00 6866 530
No. 8	00 6866 521
No. 9	00 6866 520
No. 10	00 6866 510
No. 11	00 6866 500
No. 12	00 6866 432
No. 13	00 6866 431
No. 14	00 6866 430
No. 15	00 6866 421
No. 16	00 6866 420
No. 17	00 6866 410
No. 18	00 6866 400
No. 19	00 6866 321
No. 20	00 6866 320

Gross Gemshorn 8'
    No. 21.....................00 6866 310
    No. 22.....................00 6866 300
    No. 23.....................00 6866 210
    No. 24.....................00 6866 200
    No. 25.....................00 6866 100

Harmonica (organ type) 8'
    No. 1......................00 1233 321
    No. 2......................00 1233 320
    No. 3......................00 1233 310
    No. 4......................00 1233 300
    No. 5......................00 1233 210
    No. 6......................00 1233 200
    No. 7......................00 1233 100
    No. 8......................00 1233 110
    No. 9......................00 1233 111

*Keen Strings 8'
    No. 1......................00 1476 553
    No. 2......................00 1476 552
    No. 3......................00 1476 551
    No. 4......................00 1476 550
    No. 5......................00 1476 442
    No. 6......................00 1476 441
    No. 7......................00 1476 440
    No. 8......................00 1476 331
    No. 9......................00 1476 330
    No. 10.....................00 1476 221
    No. 11.....................00 1476 220
    No. 12.....................00 1475 442
    No. 13.....................00 1475 441
    No. 14.....................00 1475 440
    No. 15.....................00 1475 331
    No. 16.....................00 1475 330
    No. 17.....................00 1475 221
    No. 18.....................00 1475 220
    No. 19.....................00 1376 553
    No. 20.....................00 1376 552

*Keen Strings 8'
    No. 21.....................00 1376 551
    No. 22.....................00 1376 550
    No. 23.....................00 1376 442
    No. 24.....................00 1376 441
    No. 25.....................00 1376 440
    No. 26.....................00 1376 331
    No. 27.....................00 1376 330
    No. 28.....................00 1376 221
    No. 29.....................00 1376 220
    No. 30.....................00 1375 442
    No. 31.....................00 1375 441
    No. 32.....................00 1375 440
    No. 33.....................00 1375 331
    No. 34.....................00 1375 330
    No. 35.....................00 1375 221
    No. 36.....................00 1375 220
    No. 37.....................00 1374 331
    No. 38.....................00 1374 330
    No. 39.....................00 1374 221
    No. 40.....................00 1374 220
    No. 41.....................00 1687 664
    No. 42.....................00 1687 553
    No. 43.....................00 1687 442
    No. 44.....................00 1687 331

*Chorus Control indispensable.

Muted 'Cello 8'
No. 1 . . . . .00 1342 020
No. 2 . . . . .00 1342 010
Muted Cone Gamba 8' 00 2475 120
Muted String 8'
No. 1 . . . . .00 2452 120
No. 2 . . . . .00 2452 020
No. 3 . . . . .00 2452 010
No. 4 . . . . .00 2452 000
Muted Viola 8'
No. 1 . . . . .00 2463 120
No. 2 . . . . .00 2463 020
No. 3 . . . . .00 2463 010
No. 4 . . . . .00 2463 000
Muted Violin 8'
No. 1 . . . . .00 1575 120
No. 2 . . . . .00 1575 020
No. 3 . . . . .00 1575 010

Nineteenth 1⅓' 00 0000 020

Octave Gemshorn 4' 00 0407 041
Octave String 4' 00 0104 064
Octave Viola 4' 00 0204 063
Orchestral String 8'
No. 1 . . . . .00 1464 321
No. 2 . . . . .00 1464 320
No. 3 . . . . .00 1464 310
No. 4 . . . . .00 1464 300
No. 5 . . . . .00 1464 210
No. 6 . . . . .00 1464 200
No. 7 . . . . .00 1464 100

Physharmonika 8'
No. 1 . . . . .00 1331 111
No. 2 . . . . .00 1331 011

Quint 5⅓' 02 0000 000
Quintviole 8' 00 4564 321

Salicional 16'
No. 1 . . . . .25 4321 000
No. 2 . . . . .25 4320 000
Salicional 8'
No. 1 . . . . .00 2453 321
No. 2 . . . . .00 2453 320
No. 3 . . . . .00 2453 310
No. 4 . . . . .00 2453 300
No. 5 . . . . .00 2453 210
No. 6 . . . . .00 2453 200
No. 7 . . . . .00 2453 100

Salicional 4'
No. 1 . . . . .00 0204 053
No. 2 . . . . .00 0204 052

Seventeenth 1⅗' 00 0000 200
Soft String 16'
No. 1 . . . . .13 3210 000
No. 2 . . . . .13 3200 000
Soft String 8'
No. 1 . . . . .00 1332 321
No. 2 . . . . .00 1332 320
No. 3 . . . . .00 1332 310
No. 4 . . . . .00 1332 300
No. 5 . . . . .00 1332 210
No. 6 . . . . .00 1332 200
No. 7 . . . . .00 1332 100
Soft String 4' 00 0103 032
Solo 'Cello 8'
No. 1 . . . . .00 3485 543
No. 2 . . . . .00 3485 432
No. 3 . . . . .00 3485 321
No. 4 . . . . .00 3485 210
No. 5 . . . . .00 3485 332
No. 6 . . . . .00 3487 223
No. 7 . . . . .00 3487 213
No. 8 . . . . .00 3487 232
No. 9 . . . . .00 3487 352
No. 10 . . . . .00 3487 342
Solo String 8'
No. 1 . . . . .00 3462 321
No. 2 . . . . .00 3465 232

Solo Viola 8′			
No. 1	00	2474	341
No. 2	00	2474	231

Solo Violin 8′			
No. 1	00	3654	323
No. 2	00	3654	324
No. 3	00	3654	322
No. 4	00	3654	231
No. 5	00	3454	323
No. 6	00	3454	324
No. 7	00	3454	322
No. 8	00	3454	231

Stentor Gamba 8′			
No. 1	00	3586	543
No. 2	00	3586	544
No. 3	00	3586	542
No. 4	00	3586	434

*String Céleste 8′			
No. 1	00	2564	411
No. 2	00	2564	311
No. 3	00	2564	211
No. 4	00	2564	111

*String Organ			
No. 1	22	5787	765
No. 2	22	5787	764
No. 3	22	5787	763
No. 4	22	5787	762
No. 5	22	5787	761
No. 6	22	5787	760
No. 7	22	5787	754
No. 8	22	5787	753
No. 9	22	5787	752
No. 10	22	5787	751
No. 11	22	5787	750
No. 12	22	5787	743
No. 13	22	5787	742
No. 14	22	5787	741
No. 15	22	5787	740
No. 16	22	5787	732
No. 17	22	5787	731
No. 18	22	5787	730
No. 19	22	5787	721
No. 20	22	5787	720
No. 21	22	5787	710
No. 22	22	5787	700
No. 23	22	5787	654
No. 24	22	5787	653
No. 25	22	5787	652
No. 26	22	5787	651
No. 27	22	5787	650
No. 28	22	5787	643
No. 29	22	5787	642
No. 30	22	5787	641
No. 31	22	5787	640
No. 32	22	5787	632
No. 33	22	5787	631
No. 34	22	5787	630
No. 35	22	5787	621

*String Organ			
No. 36	22	5787	620
No. 37	22	5787	610
No. 38	22	5787	600
No. 39	22	5787	543
No. 40	21	5787	542
No. 41	22	5787	541
No. 42	22	5787	540
No. 43	22	5787	532
No. 44	22	5787	531
No. 45	22	5787	530
No. 46	22	5787	521
No. 47	22	5787	520
No. 48	22	5787	510
No. 49	22	5787	500
No. 50	22	5787	432
No. 51	22	5787	431
No. 52	22	5787	430
No. 53	22	5787	421
No. 54	22	5787	420
No. 55	22	5787	410
No. 56	22	5787	400
No. 57	22	5787	321
No. 58	22	5787	320
No. 59	22	5787	310
No. 60	22	5787	300
No. 61	22	5787	210
No. 62	22	5787	200
No. 63	22	5787	100
No. 64	23	4767	765
No. 65	23	4767	764
No. 66	23	4767	763
No. 67	23	4767	762
No. 68	23	4767	761
No. 69	23	4767	760
No. 70	23	4767	754
No. 71	23	4767	753
No. 72	23	4767	752
No. 73	23	4767	751
No. 74	23	4767	750
No. 75	23	4767	743
No. 76	23	4767	742
No. 77	23	4767	741
No. 78	23	4767	740
No. 79	23	4767	732
No. 80	23	4767	731
No. 81	23	4767	730
No. 82	23	4767	721
No. 83	23	4767	720
No. 84	23	4767	710
No. 85	23	4767	700
No. 86	23	4767	654
No. 87	23	4767	653
No. 88	23	4767	652
No. 89	23	4767	651
No. 90	23	4767	650
No. 91	23	4767	643
No 92	23	4767	642

*Chorus Control indispensable.

*String Organ
No. 93.................23 4767 641
No. 94.................23 4767 640
No. 95.................23 4767 632
No. 96.................23 4767 631
No. 97.................23 4767 630
No. 98.................23 4767 621
No. 99.................23 4767 620
No. 100................23 4767 610
No. 101................23 4767 600
No. 102................23 4767 543
No. 103................23 4767 542
No. 104................23 4767 541
No. 105................23 4767 540
No. 106................23 4767 532
No. 107................23 4767 531
No. 108................23 4767 530
No. 109................23 4767 521
No. 110................23 4767 520
No. 111................23 4767 510
No. 112................23 4767 500
No. 113................23 4767 432
No. 114................23 4767 431
No. 115................23 4767 430
No. 116................23 4767 421
No. 117................23 4767 420
No. 118................23 4767 410
No. 119................23 4767 400
No. 120................23 4767 321
No. 121................23 4767 320
No. 122................23 4767 310
No. 123................23 4767 300
No. 124................23 4767 210
No. 125................23 4767 200
No. 126................23 4767 100

String Reed 8′
No. 1...................00 5563 321
No. 2...................00 5563 320
No. 3...................00 5563 310
No. 4...................00 5563 300
No. 5...................00 5563 210
No. 6...................00 5563 200
No. 7...................00 5563 100
Twelfth 2⅔′..............00 0020 000
Twenty-second 1′..........00 0000 002

Viola 8′
No. 1...................00 2463 332
No. 2...................00 2463 331
No. 3...................00 2463 330
No. 4...................00 2463 321
No. 5...................00 2463 320
No. 6...................00 2463 310
No. 7...................00 2463 300
No. 8...................00 2463 221
No. 9...................00 2463 210
No. 10..................00 2463 200
No. 11..................00 2463 100
Viola Aetheria 8′..........00 1233 311

*Chorus Control indispensable.

Viola à Pavillon 8′

No. 1	00 3473 321
No. 2	00 3473 320
No. 3	00 3473 310
No. 4	00 3473 300
No. 5	00 3473 210
No. 6	00 3473 200
No. 7	00 3473 100

*Viola Céleste 8′

No. 1	00 2463 222
No. 2	00 2463 111
No. 3	00 2463 011

Viola da Gamba 8′

No. 1	00 2465 432
No. 2	00 2465 431
No. 3	00 2465 430
No. 4	00 2465 421
No. 5	00 2465 420
No. 6	00 2465 410
No. 7	00 2465 400
No. 8	00 2465 321
No. 9	00 2465 320
No. 10	00 2465 310
No. 11	00 2465 300
No. 12	00 2465 210
No. 13	00 2465 200
No. 14	00 2465 100

*Viola da Gamba Céleste 8′

No. 1	00 2465 222
No. 2	00 2465 111
No. 3	00 2465 011

Viola d'Amore 8′

No. 1	00 2343 321
No. 2	00 2343 320
No. 3	00 2343 310
No. 4	00 2343 300
No. 5	00 2343 210
No. 6	00 2343 200
No. 7	00 2343 100

*Viola d'Amore Céleste 8′

No. 1	00 2343 111
No. 2	00 2343 011

Viola Phonon 8′

No. 1	00 4565 432
No. 2	00 4565 431
No. 3	00 4565 430
No. 4	00 4565 421
No. 5	00 4565 420
No. 6	00 4565 410
No. 7	00 4565 400
No. 8	00 4565 321
No. 9	00 4565 320
No. 10	00 4565 310
No. 11	00 4565 300
No. 12	00 4565 210
No. 13	00 4565 200
No. 14	00 4565 100

Viola Sorda 8′

No. 1	00 2132 210
No. 2	00 2132 200
No. 3	00 2132 100

*Viola Sorda Céleste 8′

No. 1	00 2132 111
No. 2	00 2132 011

Viola Sourdine 8′

No. 1	00 1344 210
No. 2	00 1344 200
No. 3	00 1344 100

Violetta 4′

No. 1	00 0104 053
No. 2	00 0105 053

Violin 8′

No. 1	00 2364 434
No. 2	00 2364 433
No. 3	00 2364 432
No. 4	00 2364 424
No. 5	00 2364 423
No. 6	00 2364 422
No. 7	00 2364 421
No. 8	00 2364 333
No. 9	00 2364 332
No. 10	00 2364 322
No. 11	00 2382 312
No. 12	00 2382 311
No. 13	00 2382 310
No. 14	00 2382 234
No. 15	00 2382 233
No. 16	00 2382 243
No. 17	00 2382 244
No. 18	00 2382 245
No. 19	00 2382 246
No. 20	00 2382 247
No 21	00 2476 263
No. 22	00 2476 264
No. 23	00 2476 241
No. 24	00 2476 240
No. 25	00 2476 203
No. 26	00 2476 201

*Chorus Control indispensable.

Violina 4′
No. 1.....................00 0103 064
No. 2.....................00 0103 063
Violine 16′
No. 1.....................26 3431 000
No. 2.....................26 3430 000
No. 3.....................26 3421 000
No. 4.....................26 3420 000
No. 5.....................26 3410 000
No. 6.....................26 3400 000
Voix Angélique 8′...........00 0111 010
***Voix Céleste 8′**
No. 1.....................00 2564 333
No. 2.....................00 2564 233
No. 3.....................00 2564 133
No. 4.....................00 2564 222
No. 5.....................00 2564 122
No. 6.....................00 2564 111

*Chorus Control indispensable.

UNASSIGNED BASIC STRING
NUMBER-ARRANGEMENTS FOR THE ADVANCED STUDENT

The following basic String number-arrangements have not been assigned to any particular name in the Dictionary. You may add names to them.

00 2888 532	00 2466 321	00 1587 643
00 2887 432	00 2464 211	00 1586 432
00 2886 321	00 2455 321	00 1584 321
00 2885 321	00 2443 210	00 1577 642
00 2884 210	00 2388 411	00 1574 632
00 2788 642	00 2387 531	00 1566 321
00 2787 641	00 2386 432	00 1565 431
00 2785 431	00 2384 532	00 1564 321
00 2784 321	00 2377 642	00 1554 632
00 2776 531	00 2375 321	00 1488 742
00 2775 310	00 2366 321	00 1487 642
00 2774 321	00 2344 211	00 1486 321
00 2688 742	00 1888 863	00 1484 642
00 2687 322	00 1887 431	00 1474 632
00 2685 323	00 1886 321	00 1466 532
00 2684 320	00 1885 431	00 1443 562
00 2677 431	00 1884 321	00 1388 752
00 2675 321	00 1788 321	00 1387 542
00 2674 563	00 1787 431	00 1386 542
00 2666 431	00 1786 541	00 1385 432
00 2665 310	00 1785 541	00 1384 753
00 2588 341	00 1784 563	00 1377 642
00 2587 324	00 1777 531	00 1366 532
00 2586 321	00 1776 342	00 1365 432
00 2585 310	00 1775 431	00 1355 321
00 2577 321	00 1774 251	00 1288 632
00 2576 321	00 1688 853	00 1287 632
00 2566 310	00 1686 741	00 1286 511
00 2565 431	00 1685 432	00 1285 312
00 2555 321	00 1684 634	00 1284 532
00 2554 321	00 1677 853	00 1277 632
00 2488 321	00 1676 574	00 1276 511
00 2487 532	00 1675 342	00 1275 411
00 2486 321	00 1674 352	00 1274 411
00 2485 321	00 1665 432	00 1266 311
00 2484 210	00 1664 352	00 1264 211
00 2477 310	00 1588 642	

THE FULL ORGANS

Full Great
No. 1 . . . . 74 8888 542
No. 2 . . . . 74 8888 541
No. 3 . . . . 74 8888 540
No. 4 . . . . 74 8888 431
No. 5 . . . . 74 8888 311

Full Great with Reeds
No. 1 . . . . 84 8888 854
No. 2 . . . . 84 8888 853
No. 3 . . . . 84 8888 852
No. 4 . . . . 84 8888 851
No. 5 . . . . 84 8888 850

Full Great with Mixtures
No. 1 . . . . 64 8888 563
No. 2 . . . . 64 8888 453
No. 3 . . . . 64 8888 342
No. 4 . . . . 64 8888 231
No. 5 . . . . 64 8888 121

Full Great with Reeds and
  Mixtures
No. 1 . . . . 85 8888 786
No. 2 . . . . 85 8888 675
No. 3 . . . . 85 8888 564
No. 4 . . . . 85 8888 453
No. 5 . . . . 85 8888 342

Full Accompanimental
No. 1 . . . . 31 6666 543
No. 2 . . . . 31 6666 432
No. 3 . . . . 31 6666 321
No. 4 . . . . 31 6666 210
No. 5 . . . . 31 6666 110

Full Swell
No. 1 . . . . 73 8888 543
No. 2 . . . . 73 8888 542
No. 3 . . . . 73 8888 541
No. 4 . . . . 73 8888 532
No. 5 . . . . 73 8888 531

Full Swell with Reeds
No. 1 . . . . 76 8888 664
No. 2 . . . . 76 8888 663
No. 3 . . . . 76 8888 662
No. 4 . . . . 76 8888 661
No. 5 . . . . 76 8888 653

Full Swell with Mixtures
No. 1 . . . . 67 8888 675
No. 2 . . . . 67 8888 564
No. 3 . . . . 67 8888 453
No. 4 . . . . 67 8888 342
No. 5 . . . . 67 8888 231

Full Swell with Reeds and
  Mixtures
No. 1 . . . . 86 8888 786
No. 2 . . . . 86 8888 675

Full Swell with Reeds and
  Mixtures
No. 3 . . . . 86 8888 564
No. 4 . . . . 86 8888 453
No. 5 . . . . 86 8888 342

Full Choir
No. 1 . . . . 52 7777 653
No. 2 . . . . 52 7777 652
No. 3 . . . . 52 7777 651
No. 4 . . . . 52 7777 543
No. 5 . . . . 52 7777 542

Full Choir with Mixtures
No. 1 . . . . 34 7777 675
No. 2 . . . . 34 7777 564
No. 3 . . . . 34 7777 453
No. 4 . . . . 34 7777 342
No. 5 . . . . 34 7777 231

Full Orchestral
No. 1 . . . . 87 8888 788
No. 2 . . . . 87 8888 677
No. 3 . . . . 87 8888 566
No. 4 . . . . 87 8888 455
No. 5 . . . . 87 8888 344

Full Solo
No. 1 . . . . 50 8888 765
No. 2 . . . . 50 8888 764
No. 3 . . . . 50 8888 763
No. 4 . . . . 50 8888 762
No. 5 . . . . 50 8888 761

Full Solo with Tuba Mirabilis
No. 1 . . . . 63 8888 880
No. 2 . . . . 63 8888 876
No. 3 . . . . 63 8888 875
No. 4 . . . . 63 8888 874
No. 5 . . . . 63 8888 873

Full Echo
No. 1 . . . . 31 6665 432
No. 2 . . . . 31 6665 431
No. 3 . . . . 31 6665 430
No. 4 . . . . 31 6665 421
No. 5 . . . . 31 6665 420

Full Bombarde
No. 1 . . . . 87 8878 876
No. 2 . . . . 87 8878 875
No. 3 . . . . 87 8878 874
No. 4 . . . . 87 8878 873
No. 5 . . . . 87 8878 872

Full Bombarde with Ophicleide
No. 1 . . . . 88 8888 888
No. 2 . . . . 88 8888 887
No. 3 . . . . 88 8888 886
No. 4 . . . . 88 8888 885
No. 5 . . . . 88 8888 884

THE PERCUSSIONS

(Always play staccato)

Bells 8'
   No. 1....................00 2404 002
   No. 2....................00 2004 002
   No. 3....................00 3006 003
Bells 4'....................00 0305 002
Bells 2'....................00 0004 002

Céleste Harp 8'............00 6200 000
Chimes 8'
   No. 1....................00 1600 000
   No. 2....................00 2700 000
   No. 3....................00 3800 000

(The "dying-away" effect of Chimes is obtained to a degree with the sustained tones of the organ by reducing the Expression Pedal quickly at first and immediately afterwards very slowly, after having struck the chord with the Expression Pedal depressed. Chords made up of octaves and fifths played in the upper part of the keyboard produce the best Chime-effect.)

Glockenspiel 2'
   No. 1....................00 0007 004
   No. 2....................00 0008 005

Harp 8'
   No. 1....................00 2800 000
   No. 2....................00 1800 000

Marimba 8'
   No. 1....................00 8006 000
   No. 2....................00 7004 000

Vibra-harp 8'
   No. 1....................00 6000 000
   No. 2....................00 5000 000

Xylophone 8'
   No. 1....................00 7000 070
   No. 2....................00 7000 270
   No. 3....................08 0000 080
Xylophone 4'................00 0700 040

SUGGESTED SELECTIONS FOR THE AVERAGE ORGANIST

Before the organist of average ability and the pianist who has just discovered the possibilities of the residence organ, there is a vast wealth of pleasure if the technique of the fourth and fifth grades has been mastered. Those who wish to play their organs with little or no special organ training should learn to do two things before attempting to entertain either themselves or friends:

1.   Play the Pedal keyboard in a manner that is satisfactory to the calibre of music used;
2.   Learn to draw stops appropriate to the selections.

For just the average player, the following one hundred selections have been chosen. Stops appropriate to their interpretation have been marked, but the player need not be bound by them.

Many of the selections included are not published for the organ, but may be readily adapted at the console from the vocal or piano versions.

"Classical" And "Semi-Classical" Compositions

1.   Largo from "New World Symphony", Dvořák (English Horn).
2   Overture, "Fingal's Cave", Mendelssohn (Waldflöte).
3.   Symphony No. 5, Beethoven (Allegro con brio, 00 7755 100; Andante con moto, 'Cello; Allegro, 00 7764 210).
4.   Procession of the Sardar from "Caucasian Sketches", Ippolitov-Ivanov (Principal theme on 00 4425 001).
5.   Military March in D, Schubert (10 6664 200).
6.   Nocturne from "A Midsummer Night's Dream", Mendelssohn (French Horn without Tremulant or Chorus Control).
7.   Overture to "A Midsummer Night's Dream", Mendelssohn (Orchestral Violin and also Great Organ with Reeds).
8.   Anitra's Dance from "Peer Gynt" Suite, Grieg (00 6431 000).
9.   The Beautiful Blue Danube Waltz, Strauss (10 7643 100).
10.   Morning from "Peer Gynt" Suite, Grieg (00 6700 000).
11   Chanson Triste, Tchaikovsky (00 2655 431).
12.   The Flight of the Bumble Bee, Rimsky-Korsakoff (00 5430 000)
13.   Overture from the "Nutcracker" Suite, Tchaikovsky (00 7777 321).
14.   Loure, Bach (00 2443 210).
15.   Gavotte, Gossec (00 4013 000).
16.   Minuet, Boccherini (00 1454 310).
17.   Moment Musical, Op. 74, No. 3, Schubert (00 4321 000).
18.   Gipsy Rondo, Haydn (00 2555 321).
19.   Serenade, Schubert (00 8100 000).
20.   Träumerei, Schumann (10 2543 210).
21.   Wedding March from "A Midsummer Night's Dream", Mendelssohn (Trumpets and 00 7776 210).
22.   The Swan, Saint-Saëns (00 6600 000).
23.   A Love Dream (Liebestraum), Liszt (00 3554 000).
24.   Menuet à l'Antique, Paderewski (00 1444 210).
25.   Cradle Song, Hauser (00 5000 000).

"Classical" And "Semi-Classical" Compositions

26. Ave Maria, Schubert (00 2444 200). (Play melody one octave lower than written.)
27. The Shepherd Boy, Wilson (00 3821 000).
28. Berceuse from "Jocelyn", Godard (00 4300 000).
29. March from the "Nutcracker" Suite, Tchaikovsky (Trumpets and 00 6653 100).
30. Slumber Song, Schumann (00 5555 210).
31. Andante from "Surprise" Symphony, Haydn (00 6665 321).
32. Funeral March, Chopin ('Cello or 00 7321 000).
33. See The Conquering Hero Comes, from "Judas Maccabaeus", Handel (00 8855 321).
34. A Polish Dance, Scharwenka (00 7888 680).

Operatic Excerpts

35. Coronation March from "Le Prophète", Meyerbeer (French Trumpets and 00 8877 431).
36. Prelude to Act 1, "Carmen", Bizet (20 7774 210).
37. Prelude, "Lohengrin", Wagner (00 2355 521).
38. Prelude to Act 3, "Lohengrin", Wagner (00 8888 530).
39. To The Evening Star, "Tannhäuser", Wagner ('Cello).
40. Entr'acte, "Rosamunde", Schubert (00 1455 321).
41. Prayer, "Hansel and Gretel", Humperdinck (00 3320 000).
42. I Dreamt That I Dwelt In Marble Halls, "The Bohemian Girl", Balfe (00 5650 000).
43. Elsa's Dream, "Lohengrin", Wagner (00 6654 000).
44. Ballet, "Sylvia", Delibes (00 3500 000).
45. Opening Chorus, "The Bartered Bride", Smetana (10 8886 321).
46. Waltz Song, "Romeo and Juliet", Gounod (00 4700 000).
47. Hymn to the Sun, "Le Coq d'Or", Rimsky-Korsakoff (00 5022 000).
48. 'Tis The Last Rose of Summer, "Martha", von Flotow (Clarinet).
49. The Flowers That Bloom In The Spring, "The Mikado", Sullivan (00 7764 100).
50. Bridal March, "Lohengrin", Wagner (Trumpets and 00 2402 000).
51. Glory to Egypt, "Aida", Verdi (00 7888 640).
52. Micaela's Aria, "Carmen", Bizet (Clarinet).
53. Intermezzo, "Cavalleria Rusticana", Mascagni (00 1244 321).
54. Thou Hast Spread Thy Wings To Heaven, "Lucia di Lammeimoor", Donizetti (Oboe Horn).
55. Chorus, "Per te d'immenso giubilo", "Lucia di Lammermoor", Donizetti (00 5664 210).
56. Hymn to Venus, "Tannhäuser", Wagner (00 7776 321).
57. Home To Our Mountains, "Il Trovatore", Verdi (00 6633 000).
58. The Vision Of Marguerite, "Faust", Gounod (Keen Strings).
59. The Fair, "Faust", Gounod (Great Organ with Reeds).
60. Waltz Chorus, "Faust", Gounod (Great Organ without Reeds).

Songs

61. Ciribiribin, Pestalozza (Oboe Horn or 00 8642 000).
62. Beautiful Heaven, Fernandez (00 8800 000).
63. Dark Eyes, Salami ('Cello or 00 8000 000).
64. Passing By, Purcell (00 6633 000 without Tremulant).
65. Songs My Mother Taught Me, Dvořák ('Cello or 00 4210 000).
66. Londonderry Air, Old Irish Melody (Oboe Horn) (Play melody one octave lower than written).
67. When Love Is Kind, Old Melody (00 7744 000).
68. Cradle Song, Brahms (00 6000 000 or 00 4700 000).
69. John Peel, Old English Melody (00 8753 000).
70. Drink To Me Only With Thine Eyes, Old English (00 3500 000).
71. All Through The Night, Old Welsh Air (00 5530 000).
72. Juanita (00 8410 000 or 'Cello).
73. In The Evening By The Moonlight, Bland (00 5663 000).
74. Sailing, Marks (Great Organ without Reeds).
75. Carry Me Back To Old Virginny, Bland (00 7532 000).
76. Silver Threads Among The Gold, Danks ('Cello).
77. My Old Kentucky Home, Foster (00 6543 210).
78. Old Folks At Home, Foster (00 6430 000).
79. Beautiful Dreamer, Foster (00 4500 000 or 00 8000 000).
80. In The Gloaming, Harrison (00 7000 000 or 'Cello).
81. Auld Lang Syne, Old Scotch Air (Great Organ with Reeds).
82. Deep River, American Negro Spiritual ('Cello or 00 8410 000).
83. Nobody Knows The Trouble I've Seen, American Negro Spiritual (00 8631 000).
84. Aloha Oe, Queen Liliuokalani (00 6000 000 or 00 2555 432).
85. Stars Of The Summer Night, Woodbury ('Cello or 00 2401 000).
86. Hark, Hark, The Lark, Schubert (00 4512 000).
87. I'll Sing Thee Songs Of Araby, Clay (Great Organ with Reeds).
88. Sweet And Low, Barnby (00 8300 000 or 'Cello).
89. Old Black Joe, Foster (00 5320 000).
90. O Sole Mio, di Capua (Full Swell Organ with Reeds or 00 7766 210).
91. Beautiful Isle Of The Sea, Thomas (Orchestral Violin).
92. At Pierrot's Door, French Folk-Song (00 3404 000).
93. "The Old Refrain" ('Cello or 00 4700 000).
94. Prayer Of Thanksgiving, Netherlands Tune (00 7744 000).
95. Calm As The Night, Bohm (00 5100 000).
96. For Music, Franz (00 5310 000).
97. Lo, How A Rose E'er Blooming, Praetorius (00 6633 000 without Tremulant).
98. Where'er You Walk, Handel (Full Swell Organ without Reeds).
99. America, The Beautiful, Ward (20 7887 430).
100. Steal Away, Negro Melody (00 3510 000).

INDEX

Accompaniment of voices, 26, 27
Accompanimental Diapason, 36
Accompanimental Flute, 73
Acoustics, 12, 13, 29-31
Adjusting Pre-Set keys, 15
Aeoline, 78
Aeoline Céleste, 78
Aeoline Vibrato, 78
Aeolodicon, 48
Aequalprinzipal, 36
Amorosa, 73

Baritone, 48
Basset-horn, 48
Bass Flute, 73
Bassoon, 48
Bass Open Diapason, 36
Bass Tuba, 48
Bass Violin, 78
Bass Vox Humana, 48
Bauerflöte, 73
Bell Clarinet, 16, 48
Bell Diapason, 36
Bell Gamba, 78
Bells, 91
Blockflöte, 73
Bombarde, 23, 24, 48
Bombardon, 48
Bordunalflöte, 73
Bourdon, 22, 23, 24, 73
Bourdonecho, 73
Brass Fanfare, 48, 49
Brass Trumpet, 49
Bugle, 49

Campana, 36
Cathedral Diapason, 17, 36
Céleste, 18-20, 78
Céleste Harp, 91
Célestina, 73
'Cello, 16, 17, 78
'Cello Phonon, 79
'Cello Pomposa, 79
'Cello Sordo, 79
'Cello Sordo Céleste, 79
Chalumeau, 50
Chamade, 50
Changing pitch of stop, 3, 4
Chimes, 28, 91
Chimney Flute, 73
Choir Diapason, 36
Choralbasset, 37
Chorus Control, 18-21
Chorus Diapason, 37
Chorus Reed, 50
Clarabella, 73
Claribel Flute, 73
Clarinet, 8, 10, 16, 17, 50, 51
Clarion, 51
Clarion d'Amour, 51
Clarion Sonora, 51
Clarion Tuba Harmonic, 51
Clear Flute, 73
Combining stops, 13, 14
Concert Flute, 73
Concert Piccolo, 73
Cone Flute, 73
Cone Gamba, 79
Contest between organ and or-
    chestra, 28

Contra Cathedral Diapason, 37
Contra Clarinet, 51
Contra Diapason, 37
Contra Dulciana, 79
Contra Fagotto, 51
Contra Flute, 73
Contra French Horn, 51
Contra Gamba, 79
Contra Geigen Diapason, 37
Contra Gemshorn, 79
Contra Oboe, 51
Contra Oboe Horn, 51
Contra Open Diapason, 37
Contra Posaune, 51
Contra Prinzipal, 37
Contra Saxophone, 51
Contra Solo Diapason, 37
Contra Trombone, 51
Contra Trumpet, 51
Contra Tuba, 51
Contra Vox Humana, 3, 51
Cordedain, 73
Cor de Nuit, 73
Cornet, 51
Cornet à Pavillon, 52
Cornet d'Amour, 52
Corno d'Amore, 52
Corno di Bassetto, 52
Corno Dolce, 52
Corno Flute, 52
Cornopean, 52
Cromorne, 53
Cro Orlo en Chamade, 53

Dance orchestra, 28,
Diapason, 3, 8, 9, 18, 22, 26,
    27, 37
Diapason Chorus, 16, 18, 22, 23,
    37
Diapason Fifteenth, 37
Diapason Magna, 37
Diapason Nineteenth, 37
Diapason Octave Quint, 37
Diapason Phonon, 37
Diapason Profunda, 38
Diapason Quint, 38
Diapason Seventeenth, 38
Diapason Sonora, 38
Diapason Twelfth, 38
Diapason Twenty-second, 38
Divinare, 73
Dolcan, 73
Doppelflöte, 73
Doppelrohrflöte, 73
Doppelrohrgedeckt, 73
Doppelspitzflöte, 73
Douple Clarinet, 53
Double Diapason, 38
Double French Horn, 53
Double Melodia, 73
Double Oboe, 53
Double Oboe Horn, 53
Double Saxophone, 53
Double Trumpet, 53
Doublette, 38
Double Tuba, 53
Double Tuba Harmonic, 53
Double Viola Diapason, 38
Double Violin Diapason, 38

Double Vox Humana, 3, 53
Dulcet, 79
Dulcian, 53
Dulciana, 16, 17, 22, 79
Duophone, 73
Duplicate number-arrange-
    ments, 3

Echo Bourdon, 73
Echo 'Cello, 80
Echo 'Cello Céleste, 80
Echo Diapason, 17, 38
Echo Dulcet, 80
Echo Dulciana, 80
Echoflöte, 22, 73
Echo Gamba, 80
Echo Gemshorn, 80
Echo Oboe, 53
Echo Violin, 22, 80
Echo Waldhorn, 53
Egyptian Bazu, 53
Egyptian Horn, 53
Endings for number-arrange-
    ments, 12, 13
English Diapason, 38
English Horn, 10, 16, 17, 53
English Tuba, 53
Erzähler, 80
Ethereal Violin, 17, 80
Ethereal Violin Céleste, 80
Euphone, 53
Euphonium, 53
Expression Pedal, 4, 21, 22

Fagotto, 53
Families of organ tone, 3, 8, 9
Fanfare, 17, 54
Feldflöte, 74
Fernflöte, 74
Field Trumpet, 54
Fife, 74
Fifteenth, 38, 74
"Fifth" harmonic controller, 6
Flachflöte, 74
Flageolet, 74
Flageolet Harmonique, 74
Flautino, 74
Flautone, 74
Flue Twelfth, 38
Flügel Horn, 55
Flute, 3, 8, 10, 11, 12, 26, 31,
    73-75
Flûte à Pavillon, 38
Flûte d'Amour, 74
Forest Flute, 74
Foundation, 3, 8, 9, 36-47
French Bugle, 55
French Horn, 8, 16, 17, 28, 55
French Trumpet, 16, 56
Full Accompanimental, 16, 90
Full Bombarde, 22, 90
Full Choir, 90
Full Echo, 90
Full Flute, 74
Full Great, 16, 17, 90
Full Orchestral, 16, 90
Full Organs, 3, 8, 14, 18, 22, 90
Full Solo, 90
Full Swell, 16, 17, 90

Gamba, 22, 80
Gamba Celesta, 80
Gambenbass, 80
Gambette, 80
Gedecktflöte, 74
Geigen Diapason, 38, 39
Geigen Octave, 39
Gemshorn, 8, 11, 81
Gemshorn Céleste, 81
German Gamba, 81
Glockenspiel, 91
Gothic Diapason, 39
Grand Diapason, 39
Grand Diapason Chorus, 39
Grand Ophicleide, 56
Grand Prinzipal, 39
Grand Violin, 81
Gross 'Cello, 81, 82
Gross Diapason, 39
Grossflöte, 74
Gross Gamba, 82
Grossgedeckt, 74
Gross Gemshorn, 82, 83
Gross Trumpet, 56, 57

Harmonica, 83
Harmonic controllers, 4-7, 22, et passim
Harmonic Diapason, 39, 40
Harmonic Flute, 74
Harmonic Oboe, 57
Harmonic Piccolo, 74
Harmonic Trumpet, 57
Harmonic Tuba, 58
Harp, 91
Heckelphone, 58
Hellflöte, 74
Hohlflöte, 74
Hohlflötenbass, 74
Hohlschelle, 74
Home installations, 30, 31
Horn Diapason, 22, 40-42
Humangedeckt, 74
Hunting Horn, 58
Hymns, 17

Jubalflöte, 74

Keen Strings, 16, 83
Keraulophone, 16, 74
Kinura, 58
Kleingedeckt, 74
Kleinprinzipal, 42

Labial Tuba, 58, 59
Larigot, 42
Lieblichbordun, 74
Lieblichflöte, 74
Lieblichgedeckt, 74

Magic Flute, 74
Main Tone Generator, 31, 32
Major Diapason, 42
Major Flute, 16, 74
Making new number-arrangements, 7, 8, 12, 13
Marimba, 91
Mellophone, 59
Melodia, 74
Military Fanfare, 59
Minor Diapason, 42
Minor Flute, 74
Mixtures, 14

Model E, 17
Musette, 59
Musette Mirabilis, 59
Muted 'Cello, 84
Muted Cone Gamba, 84
Muted String, 84
Muted Viola, 84
Muted Violin, 84

Nachthorn, 74
Nazard, 42, 74
Nineteenth, 42, 74, 84
"Nineteenth" harmonic controller, 6
Number-arrangements, 3, 4, 6-13, et passim

Oboe, 10, 16, 20, 59
Oboe d'Amore, 59
Oboe Flute, 74
Oboe Horn, 59
Oboe Major, 59
Octave, 42
Octave Flute, 74
Octave Gemshorn, 84
"Octave" harmonic controller, 6
Octave Harmonic Diapason, 42
Octave Major Diapason, 42
Octave Minor Diapason, 42
Octave Oboe, 59
Octave Phonon, 42
Octave Quint, 42
Octave String, 84
Octave Viola, 84
"Off" position of harmonic controllers, 4
Open Diapason, 9, 16-18, 22, 42, 43
Open Flute, 16, 74
Open Quint, 44
Operatic arias, 16
Ophicleide, 22, 59
Orchestra, 28
Orchestral Flute, 16, 74
Orchestral Oboe, 59, 60
Orchestral Piccolo, 74
Orchestral String, 84
Orchestral Trumpet, 60, 61
Oriental Reed, 61
Outdoor playing, 28

Parts of console, 2
Pastorita, 74
Pedal Harmonic-Controllers, 22
Pedal Keyboard, 24-26, 30
Pedal Organ, 30
Pedal Solo Unit, 23, 24
Percussions, 91
Philomela, 74
Physharmonica, 61
Physharmonika, 84
Piccolo, 3, 74
Piccolo d'Amour, 74
Playing with orchestra or band, 28
Portunalflöte, 74
Posaune, 61
Post Horn, 61
Pre-Set keys, 4, 7, 14-17
Pre-Set pistons, 17
Prestant, 44
Prinzipal, 44

Prinzipalflöte, 74
Proportion in number-arrangements, 4, 7, 11
Pyramidflöte, 74

Querflöte, 74
Quint, 44, 74, 84
Quintadena, 74
Quintaten, 74
Quint Diapason, 44
Quint Flute, 75
Quintviole, 84

Rauschflöte, 75
Rauschpfeife, 75
Rauschquinte, 75
Reed, 3, 8-10, 20 22, 27, 31, 48-72
Reed Chorus, 8, 22, 23, 62
Resources of Hammond Organ, 8
Reverberation time, 29-31
Reverberation Unit, 31
Ripienflöte, 75
Rohrflöte, 75

Salicional, 16, 84
Sanftflöte, 75
Sarrusophone, 62
Saxophone, 8, 63
Schöngedeckt, 75
Schutz Diapason, 44
Selective Vibrato system, 21
Septadecima, 44
Seraphonflöte, 75
Seventeenth, 44, 75, 84
"Seventeenth" harmonic controller, 6
Sforzando effects, 21
Sifflöte, 75
Soave, 75
Soft String, 84
Solo 'Cello, 84
Solo Diapason, 44
Solo String, 84
Solo Tuba, 63
Solo Viola, 85
Solo Violin, 85
Solo Vox Humana, 64
Spillflöte, 75
Spinet, The Hammond, 33, 34
Spire Flute, 75
Spitzflöte, 75
Stentor Diapason, 44
Stentorflöte, 75
Stentor Gamba, 85
Stentorphone, 17, 75
Stopped Diapason, 44, 75
Stopped Flute, 11, 16, 17, 75
String, 3, 8, 11, 20, 78-89
String Céleste, 85
String Organ, 8, 17, 23, 85, 86
String Reed, 86
Suabe Flute, 75
Sub Bass, 75
"Sub-octave" harmonic controller, 6
Subprinzipal, 45
Suggested selections for the organist, 92
Super Octave, 45, 75
Super Octave Flute, 75

"Super-octave" harmonic controller, 6
Super Octave Tierce, 45
"Super Super-octave" harmonic controller, 6
Swell Diapason, 45
Symphony themes, 16

Tertian, 45
Tibia, 75
Tibia Angusta, 75
Tibia Bifara, 75
Tibia Clausa, 17, 75
Tibia Dura, 16, 75
Tibia Flute, 75
Tibia Major, 75
Tibia Minor, 75
Tibia Mollis, 75
Tibia Octave, 75
Tibia Plena, 75
Tibia Profunda, 75
Tibia Rex, 75
Tibia Rurestris, 75
Tibia Sylvestris, 75
Tibia Vulgaris, 75
Tierce, 45, 75
Tierce Diapason, 45
"Toe-space", 25, 26
Traversflöte, 75
Tremulant, 18, 30
Tromba, 64
Tromba Clarion, 64

Trombone, 64
Trompette en Chamade, 64
Trumpet, 8-10, 16, 20, 28, 31, 64
Trumpet Fanfare, 64, 65
Trumpet Imperial, 65
Tuba, 8, 10, 16, 20, 65-67
Tuba Chorus, 67
Tuba d'Amore, 68
Tuba Imperial, 68
Tuba Magna, 68, 69
Tuba Major, 69
Tuba Minor, 69
Tuba Mirabilis, 16, 70
Tuba Sonora, 22, 70
Twelfth, 45, 75, 86
"Twelfth" harmonic controller, 6
Twelfth Major, 45
Twelfth Minor, 45
Twenty-second, 75, 86
Unassigned number-arrangements, 46, 72, 75, 89
Unda Maris, 17, 75
"Unison" harmonic controller, 6
Use of Dictionary, 3-4, 6-8

Vibra-harp, 91
Viola, 86
Viola Aetheria, 86
Viola à Pavillon, 87
Viola Céleste, 87
Viola da Gamba, 87
Viola da Gamba Céleste, 87

Viola d'Amore, 87
Viola d'Amore Céleste, 87
Viola Diapason, 45
Viola Phonon, 87
Viola Sorda, 87
Viola Sorda Céleste, 87
Viola Sourdine, 87
Violetta, 87
Violin, 87
Violina, 88
Violin Diapason, 45
Violine, 88
Voce Flebile, 75
Vogelflöte, 75
Voix Angélique, 88
Voix Céleste, 88
Voix Séraphique, 75
Vox Humana, 8, 71

Waldflöte, 75
Waldhorn, 71
Wienerflöte, 75
Willow Flute, 75
Wood Diapason, 45
Wooden Open Flute, 75, 76
Wooden Stopped Flute, 76
Wood-winds, 8

Xylophone, 91

Zartflöte, 76